# JAPAN IN THE YEAR 2000

## Preparing Japan for an Age of Internationalization, the Aging Society and Maturity

**Long-Term Outlook Committee,
Economic Council
Economic Planning Agency**

## The **Japan Times**, Ltd.

ISBN4-7890-0197-0

First edition: January 1983
Second printing: February 1984
Third printing: May 1985

Original Japanese-language edition *Nisen-nen no Nihon* compiled by the Economic Planning Agency. Copyright © 1982 by the Long-Term Outlook Committee. English version translated by The Japan Times, Ltd.

Published by The Japan Times, Ltd.
5-4, Shibaura 4-chome, Minato-ku, Tokyo 108

Printed in Japan

# Preface

Japan's economic society is about to undergo a major change as the country approaches the 21st century.

At this juncture, it is of immense importance to study the direction of Japan's economic society from a long-term perspective and to point out the problems that will occur in that perspective as well as to clarify what type of economic society Japan should seek to realize in the future.

To that end, the Economic Council set up the Long-Term Outlook Committee in May 1981. Since then, the committee has been studying the nation's long-term perspectives into the 21st century with as many as 128 prominent figures in various fields taking part. The present report represents the result of this study.

As pointed out in the report, Japan's economic society will have to solve a host of problems in the process of coming changes as typified by internationalization, the aging society and the maturing of society. I believe it imperative to make a correct analysis of the problems that will occur from now on and take appropriate steps to cope with them in order to hand over a dynamic economic society to the next generation.

I should like to take this opportunity of expressing my deep gratitude to Chairman Saburo Okita and the members of the committee for their dedicated efforts. At the same time, I am hopeful that this report will serve as important reference material for studying the course of Japan's economic society in the years ahead.

July 1982

Toshio Komoto
Minister of State
for Economic Planning

# About This Report

For about a year since May last year, as many as 128 experts have met a total of 182 times to conduct energetic debates and to study from an open point of view. As a result, we have now made out a report regarding the course of Japan's economic society in the next two decades up to the 21st century.

Twenty years ago in 1960, the Economic Council also undertook a study on the nation's long-term outlook. In those days, Japan was entering a period of high growth, and starting to catch up with the United States and Western European nations with great rapidity. By contrast, this latest study on the long-term outlook has been undertaken at a time when Japan is going to enter what may be called a "post-catching up" period in the new current of the times as typified by internationalization, the aging society and the maturing society. The background of the times and the nature of the problems have thus changed entirely between the two studies. Nevertheless, both were conducted at great turning points in Japan's economic society and as such, have immense significance.

An accurate prediction of the long-term course of an economic society is far from easy in view of increasing uncertainties. Nevertheless, it is considered important to grasp the general direction of changes society is expected to undergo and to take necessary measures to cope with such changes as soon as possible. This long-term outlook may well be termed a map of the next two decades. We hope that it will serve as important material in the choice of the course Japan should follow from now on just as a map is essential for trekking in mountains.

Lastly, I would like to repeat my deep gratitude to all the members of the Committee for their close cooperation.

July 1982

Saburo Okita
Chairman, Long-Term Outlook Committee,
Economic Council

# CONTENTS

# LIST OF FIGURES AND TABLES

vii

# Introduction

Our ears have already started to listen for the footsteps of the 21st century. Japan's economic society has so far gone through various vicissitudes. In the remaining two decades of the 20th century and the succeeding 21st century, what sort of economic society is in store for us?

Since the Meiji Era, the Japanese people have been exerting tremendous efforts for modernization with the common objective of catching up with the developed nations in the West. Fortunately, favored by propitious conditions both at home and abroad, Japan has achieved an economic advance without parallel in the world, now accounting for 10% of the world economy.

Nonetheless, a series of changes in both internal and external conditions for Japan as typified by a change in the international economic order with the United States as the core, limitations on natural resources and energy, and the progress of aging in society, is considered bound to have no small impact on the course of Japan's economic society in a long-term perspective as well.

On the other hand, as regards the direction of the course Japan should pursue, it has become difficult to follow the example of the developed nations as in the past. The situation is such that Japan must grope for a path of its own.

The coming years until the 21st century are believed to constitute a major turning point from a historical point of view.

Accordingly, it is considered imperative to take up the coming 20 years or so until the 21st century as a subject of study, to examine the direction of a change in Japan's economic society from a long-term point of view, to point out those problems which would emerge in the process of such a change and at the same time, to study what type of economic society Japan should seek to realize in the future, with a view to contributing to the formation of a consensus among the nation.

The latest study on the long-term outlook was undertaken in awareness of the above-mentioned necessity. For that purpose, the Long-Term Outlook Committee (chaired by Saburo Okita) was set up by the Economic Council on May 18, 1981 as a body under the General Committee. Moreover, since the study covered all aspects of the economic society, six subcommittees and various study groups were set up. In the drawing up of the final report, discussion was conducted by the Drafting Advisory Group.

As many as 128 experts in various fields took part in the study and conducted serious discussions for about a year.

This report, partly because of its nature as a long-term outlook, is not a recommendation made out at the request of the Government. Rather, it represents the result of debate and study by the members of the Long-Term Outlook Committee, who offered their own views from their respective standpoints in regard to the future of Japan's economic society. Accordingly, the report differs in nature from the Government's economic plan. However, we are hopeful that it will prove helpful as an item of important reference data when the Government and various strata of the nation consider a desirable pattern for the economic society in a long-term perspective.

# Chapter 1 Japan's Economic Society at an Historic Turning Point

What position can the period of about 20 years until the 21st century, which will be taken up in this work on the long-term outlook, be given in the long-term perspective? Before starting work on the long-term outlook, we would like to look back on the past progress of Japan's economic society from a historical point of view, define the position of the next 20 years or so, and thereby clarify the significance of the work on the long-term outlook.

## Section 1 Long-Term Trends for Japan's Economic Society

If we take a general look at the long-term tendencies of Japan's population, economic growth rate and international position, it is considered that Japan now finds itself at a very important point in the history of its economic society with less than 20 years to go before the 21st century, and that the next two decades will constitute a historic turning point in Japan's economic society in diverse senses.

### 1. Population
— Transition to Society of Stable Population at High Age Level —

[Japan's Population in Long-Term Perspective]
It was only recently that the Japanese population reached the 100 million level. In this land, a total of about 500 million people are presumed to have been engaged in economic activity since the dawn of history. Of them, about 300 million lived before the end of the 19th century, whereas about 200 million people or as much as about 40 percent of the total have inhabited the land during only 80 years of the 20th century.

Since the Meiji Restoration, Japan has experienced a rapid growth of population. Its population, which stood at 34 million in the early days of the Meiji Era, about doubled in 70 years, and shot up 3.4-fold to

117 million in 1980 or about 110 years later. In the meantime, there was the "baby boom" after World War II (See Figure 1-1-1).

**Fig. 1-1-1   Population Trends since the Meiji Era and the Forecast for Future Trends**

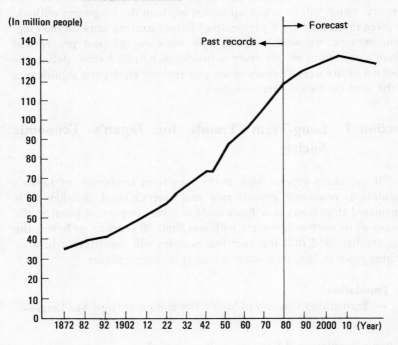

**Sources:**   Past records — Bank of Japan's Statistics Bureau "Japan's Principal Economic Statistics since Meiji"; Statistics Bureau of the Prime Minister's Office "Census"; Forecast — Based on medium variant in the "Future Population Projections for Japan by Sex-Age for 1980-2080" by the Institute of Population Problems, Health and Welfare Ministry.

[Shift to Society of Stable Population]

However, from the trends of the birth rate and the death rate in recent years, it may be considered that the period of fast population growth since the Meiji Era has come to a close and that Japan will henceforth head gradually for a phase of stable population.

To analyze the past relationship between the birth rate and the death rate (See Figure 1-1-2), the population increase from the Meiji Era to World War II resulted primarily from the rise in the birth rate, showing a pattern of many births and many deaths. But after World War II, the growth pattern changed to many births and fewer deaths through the combination of a steep rise in the birth rate during the "baby boom" and a drop in the death rate. Then the pattern shifted to fewer births and fewer deaths, owing to a fall in the birth rate. More

**Fig. 1-1-2  Trends for the Birth Rate and Death Rate**

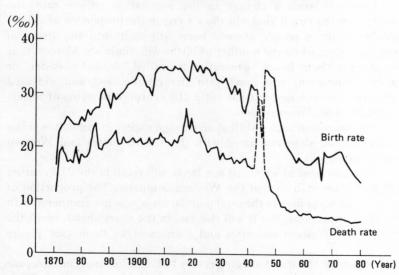

**Sources:** Bank of Japan's Statistics Bureau "Japan's Principal Economic Statistics since Meiji" for 1872-1899 and 1944-1946; Health and Welfare Ministry "Vital Statistics" for other years.

recently, the birth rate has further declined, and the pace of population growth has tended to slow down.

The prospective trends of the population may be projected in a number of ways, depending on how one looks at the future trend of the birth rate. But even assuming that the birth rate picks up somewhat, the population will conceivably hit a peak shortly after the year 2000, then show a gradual downtrend and finally head for stability.

This pattern of sharp population increase, followed by stability, is already seen in developed nations in Western Europe and North America. The historical pattern of vital statistics in all major developed nations shows that the growth of population has slowed because of a fall in the birth rate. Basically, Japan's population is also expected to follow a similar pattern.

[Shift to Advanced-Age Society]

Owing to such a change in the population growth rate, the structure of the population will show a rise in the proportion of elderly people, as those people already born will shift into the strata of advanced ages, while the number of births will diminish. Moreover, as the postwar "baby boom" generation (so-called "dankai-no-sedai" or Lump Generation) will move into the middle-aged and old-aged categories between now and the early 21st century, the aging of society will gather added momentum.

The process of such a shift to an old-age society in Japan has major characteristics when compared with the United States and Western European nations.

First, the level of advanced age Japan will reach in the 21st century will be higher than that of the Western countries. The proportion of people aged 65 or over to the total population is now low compared with the Western nations. But it will rise fast in the years ahead, reach the level of the Western countries and then overtake them (See Figure 1-1-3).

Secondly, the speed of aging is very fast. For instance, in European nations, the rise in proportion of people aged 65 or over from 7% to 14% took as long as 45-135 years. But in the case of Japan, it was only 26 years.

Two factors are recognizable behind these characteristics of Japan's population aging. Unlike Western countries, Japan has had to

**Fig. 1-1-3  An International Comparison of Aging Populations (Trends for Populations Aged 65 or Over)**

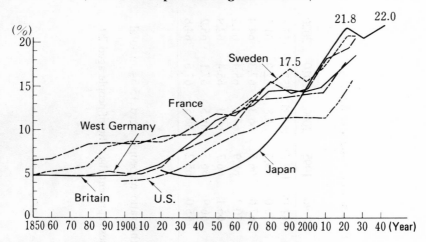

**Sources:**  Foreign countries — U.N. "The Aging of Populations and Its Economic and Social Implications" (1956) and U.N. "Demographic Yearbook" up to 1970; U.N. "Demographic Indicators by Countries as Assessed in 1980: Medium Variant" for 1990 and after; each country's statistics and U.N. data 1976-1978 for 1980.

Japan — Statistics Bureau of the Prime Minister's Office "Census" up to 1980; Institute of Population Problems of the Health and Welfare Ministry "Future Population Projections for Japan by Sex-Age for 1980-2080 (November 1981) (medium variant used).

experience at one stroke both (1) the process of change in the birth rate, which forms a common trend (degree of change is higher than in the Western nations) and (2) the process of the postwar "baby boom."

[Change in Productive-Age Population]

Thus, the aging of the population makeup is bound to progress from now on. But it is worth noting that there will be a considerable difference in the composition of the population between the next 20

**Table 1-1-4  An International Comparison of the Ratio of Productive-Age Population**

(In %)

| Nation Year | 1950 | 1960 | 1970 | 1980 | 1990 | 1995 | 2000 | 2010 | 2020 |
|---|---|---|---|---|---|---|---|---|---|
| Japan | (49.4) | (54.3) | (60.3) | (60.4) | (61.9) | (62.5) | (61.3) | (57.2) | (55.1) |
| France | 59.6 | 64.1 | 68.9 | 67.4 | 70.0 | 69.3 | 66.8 | 62.9 | 61.5 |
| West Germany | 65.9 | 62.0 | 62.3 | 64.0 | 67.0 | 66.5 | 66.3 | 67.3 | 64.4 |
| Sweden | 67.3 | 67.8 | 63.7 | 66.3 | 70.3 | 68.9 | 67.8 | 65.4 | 64.1 |
| Britain | 66.3 | 66.0 | 65.5 | 64.3 | 66.1 | 66.7 | 67.0 | 65.4 | 62.9 |
| U.S. | 66.9 | 65.1 | 62.8 | 64.3 | 66.9 | 66.5 | 66.5 | 67.1 | 65.2 |

**Notes:**

1. **Sources:** Same as Fig. 1-1-3.
2. The ratio of productive-age population is the ratio of people aged 15-64 to total population.
3. In the case of Japan, the figures in parentheses represent the ratio of people aged 20-64 to total population.

years and the years from 2000 on. During the two decades up to the 21st century, the ratio of productive-age population to the total population (Table 1-1-4) will show little change from the present ratio. Rather, it will go up in the immediate future. But from the 21st century, the ratio will decline fast. If the total population is divided into three strata — that is, young people (age 0-14), productive-age people (15-64) and people aged 65 or over, the ratio of productive-age people to the total population in Japan has been high compared with the Western nations, partly because of the high rate of population increase. From now on, the ratio of productive-age population will show little change for some time because the decrease in young people and the increase in people aged 65 or over will counterbalance each other. However, with the advent of the 21st century, the number of young people will cease to decline, while that of people aged 65 or over will continue to swell. As a result, the ratio of productive-age population will start to fall off.

The same can be said even if the ages 20 to 64 are regarded as productive ages in view of the fact that nearly 100% of lower secondary school graduates now enter upper secondary school.

In other words, the fact that the ratio of productive-age population is high means that the index of dependent population (the ratio of the total of young people and people aged 65 or over to the productive-age population) is low. From a macro point of view, this means that the burden carried by the productive-age population is light.

From the above-mentioned change in the population, it may be said that the ensuing 20 years will constitute a valuable period left for us to ensure a soft landing on the advanced-age society in the coming 21st century.

## 2. Economic Growth
### — Age of Medium Growth —

[Economic Growth since Meiji]

Since the Meiji Era, Japan has been treading the path of economic growth centered on industrialization.

By and large, the Japanese economy has continued to enjoy a high growth rate, since the Meiji Era though accompanied by cycles of good and bad times (See Figure 1-1-5). The growth rate averaged about 3% a year from the Meiji Restoration to 1900. It rose to about 6% thanks to a

**Fig. 1-1-5 Real Economic Growth Rate Trends since Meiji**

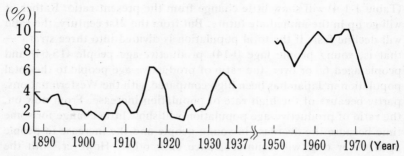

**Notes:**

1. **Source:** Takahusa Nakamura "Japanese Economy — Its Growth and Structure."

2. The average growth rates for a total of seven years — namely, the particular year and three-year periods each before and after that — are plotted.

boom generated by World War I. After that, the rate dropped to the 2% level owing to the Showa Panic, but with the advent of the 1930s, it rallied to the 5% level amid the rapid growth of heavy and chemical industries in the nation's industrial fabric.

The average annual growth stood at 3.1% from 1885 to 1940. This exceeded the growth pace of Western European nations, though falling short of that of the United States. During this period, the Japanese economy was walking a path of self-sustained industrialization, leaving behind the stage of developing nation with primitive accumulation through agriculture as leverage.

Nevertheless, World War II dealt a severe blow to the Japanese economy.

[Age of High Growth]

Later, Japan started to tread the path of reconstruction from scratch under its new economic and social systems, plunging into an era of high growth.

After World War II, Japan's growth rate increased markedly, and the average annual growth was as high as 9.5% from 1955 to 1973.

This was apparently ascribable to (1) the process of rapid reconstruction and the reform of the economic and social systems after the war, (2) the process of filling the wide gap with developed nations in such aspects as technology, national life and employment structure, (3) the high savings ratio of the nation and the Government's economic policy of attaching importance to growth and (4) propitious international conditions, including the expansion of world trade, inexpensive petroleum resources and a peaceful international environment.

This rapid growth, accompanied by the progress of industrialization, led to the sophistication of the industrial structure, and Japan's position in the world economy rose considerably. Japan's GNP per capita also grew almost to the level of developed nations, while national life became affluent (See Figure 1-1-6).

This period of high growth may be defined as a period for catching up with the economic level of developed nations in Europe and the United States.


[Change in Growth Rate and Shift to Medium Growth]

However, from the 1970s, the Japanese economy shifted from high growth to medium growth (See Figure 1-1-7).

The change in the growth pace was conceivably influenced by various factors, such as a change in the international environment, including the energy situation, a rise in the average age of capital, and a change in growth-mindedness. Basically, however, it meant the end of high growth, which constituted a catching-up process.

Nowadays, the idea of such medium growth is believed to have already taken root in the perception of the bulk of economic entities, leading them to behave from now on with medium growth as their premise.


[Current State of Japanese Economy]

Of late, the Japanese economy has been marked by the slow growth of domestic demand and economic frictions with foreign countries. Moreover, the reconstruction of the national finances has become an urgent task because of the massive deficit. For the present, it is necessary to solve those problems in order to cope with various

## Fig. 1-1-6 Trends for Real GNP and Population since Meiji

### (1) Real GNP and Population

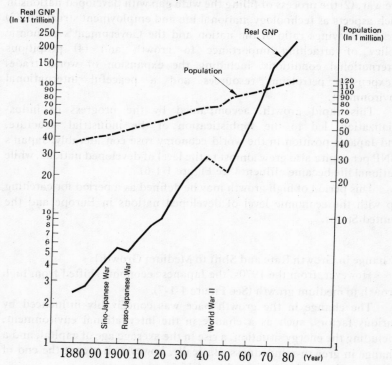

**Notes:**

1. **Sources:** Real GNP — Calculated by Planning Bureau of the Economic Planning Agency on the basis of Bank of Japan "Japan's Principal Economic Statistics (Okawa Estimation)," Economic Planning Agency "Annual Report on National Income Statistics," etc. Population — Statistics Bureau of the Prime Minister's Office "Census," etc.

2. Real GNP is based on the 1980 price level.

3. The per-capita GNP of other nations for 1980 was calculated by the Planning Bureau of the Economic Planning Agency on the basis of IMF "IFS" and U.N. estimates.

## (2) Real GNP Per Capita

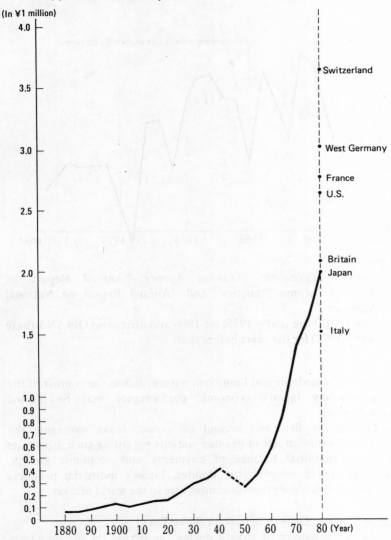

(In ¥1 million)

- Switzerland
- West Germany
- France
- U.S.
- Britain
- Japan
- Italy

1880　90　1900　10　20　30　40　50　60　70　80 (Year)

## Fig. 1-1-7 Recent Trends for Real GNP Growth Rates

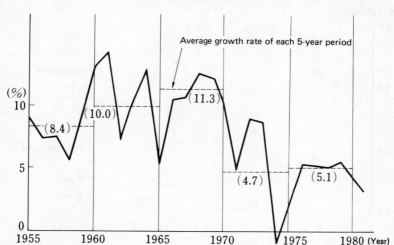

**Notes:**
1. **Sources:** Economic Planning Agency "Annual Report on National Income Statistics" and "Annual Report on National Accounts."
2. New SNA (base year—1975) for 1966 and after, and Old SNA (base year—1970) for the years before that.

problems of a medium and long-term nature. But in the context of the world economy Japan's economic performance may be termed relatively good.

During the first and second oil crises, Japan overcame the "trilemma" situation ahead of other nations regarding such aspects as prices, international balance of payments and economic growth, displaying superb adaptability. Besides, Japan's industrial products centering on machinery remain competitive in the world market.

[Age of Medium Growth to Last for Some Time]

As to the pattern of growth during the period for the long-term outlook, a detailed study will be made in Chapter 2. Basically, however, considering such factors as Japan's ability to develop technologies, a higher savings ratio than developed nations and the high ratio of productive-age population, Japan will be able to continue a somewhat higher growth rate (medium growth) than other developed countries, if it copes properly with changes in both internal and external conditions hereafter. In order to settle employment and other problems which will confront us in future, it is desirable to give full play to the vitality of the economy.

From the foregoing, the period until the 21st century may be defined as an age of medium growth for Japan. When viewed from the angle of growth, it will be necessary in the ensuing 20 years to take full advantage of economic vitality and cope with problems which will face the nation amid the medium growth of the economy.

## 3. International Position
—Internationally More Open Economic Society—

[Past Rise in International Position]

In the past process of catching-up fast, Japan has rapidly gained in international stature.

Japan's share of world GNP stood at a mere 2% or so in 1955, but increased rapidly in the process of high growth, reaching almost 10% in 1980 (See Table 1-1-8).

### Table 1-1-8 The Trends for National Shares in World GNP
(In %)

| Nation    Year | 1955 | 1960 | 1970 | 1978 | 1980 |
|---|---|---|---|---|---|
| Japan | 2.2 | 2.9 | 6.0 | 10.0 | 9.0 |
| U.S. | 36.3 | 33.7 | 30.2 | 21.8 | 21.5 |
| EC | 17.5 | 17.5 | 19.3 | 20.2 | 22.4 |
| USSR | 13.9 | 15.2 | 15.9 | 13.0 | 11.6 |
| China | 4.4 | 4.7 | 4.9 | 4.6 | 4.7 |
| World total | 100.0 | 100.0 | 100.0 | 100.0 | 100.0 |
| (In $1 billion) | (1,100) | (1,500) | (3,250) | (9,660) | (12,215) |

**Sources:** U.S. Government "International Economic Report of the President" (1977) for 1955-1970, and U.S. Government "Economic Report of the President" (1980, 1982) for 1978 and after.

Japan's position also rose phenomenally fast in the fields of trade and industrial production. Japan's share in world trade reached 7.3% in 1980. As for imports of resources, Japan's share was as large as 40.5% for iron ore, 30.0% for coal, 20.7% for soybeans, 14.3% for crude steel and 12.0% for wheat.

On the other hand, the world economy is becoming increasingly multipolarized, as evidenced by the relative fall in the economic position of the United States and the rise of oil-producing nations and newly industrializing countries. Under these circumstances, Japan's position and role in the world are becoming acknowledged more and more because of its fast-expanding shares.

Furthermore, in recent years, Japan has maintained a relatively good economic performance amid the stagnation of the world economy in the wake of the oil crisis. As a result, the rising relative position of the nation has been brought into still bolder relief.

[Japan Living in World]

As noted above, Japan's existence is gradually taking on great significance for the world. On the other hand, the world economy has been and will undoubtedly continue to be of great significance for Japan.

The advance of the Japanese economy after World War II was made possible by the development of the relationship of interdependence with other countries amid the generally smooth expansion of the world economy.

For Japan, which is short of natural resources, the existence of a peaceful and dynamic world economy is an indispensable prerequisite for economic development.

[Stagnant World Economy]

In recent years, however, the world economy has been affected by the economic stagnation in developed industrial states due to "stagflation," while developing nations have also continued to be gripped by economic difficulties, such as accumulated debts. Moreover, amid the rising tide of protectionism, stabilization of the international economic order is called for in the fields of trade and the monetary system. For example, the maintenance and strengthening of the free trading system, and the stable management of the floating exchange rate system.

It is first of all essential to overcome those problems facing us in order to open up a bright vista for the world economy.

[Future Relations Between the World and Japan]

If Japan maintains a relatively high pace of growth among developed nations, its position in the world will keep on rising gradually, though not as fast as in the past. And, amid the further multipolarization of the world economy, Japan will have to play an increasingly important role therein in order to solve the problems confronting it.

As Japan's international position has risen so rapidly, the gap between its economic strength and international contribution has widened. Henceforth, it will become necessary to fill such a gap and fulfill its role in an internationally balanced manner befitting the nation's position.

At the same time, Japan will be called upon to build a more open, international economic society.

As noted above, Japan has in the past maintained a passive attitude of relying on the world economy for its development. From now on, however, Japan should conduct itself positively for the stable development of the world economy, and this will serve Japan's own interests as well. Japan is also expected to enter a new stage in international relations.

## Section 2   New Grand Design Called For

As seen in the previous section, the coming period until the 21st century will be a major turning point for Japan in view of its population, economic growth and international position. Under these circumstances, Japan will face great difficulties in future if it cannot get rid of old ideas, systems and practices. Now is the time to come up with a "grand design" that will present a new course and strategy in a long-term perspective.

### 1.   Development Stage of Japan's Economic Society

The reason Japan is facing a turning point from a long-term point of view is that basically, Japan's economic society has entered a new stage of development, which is different from the past.

That is, Japan was once in a stage of catching up with developed nations, which was marked by a high population growth rate, a high rate of economic growth due to this "catching-up" and a weak awareness of Japan's position and responsibility in the international economic community.

Nevertheless, Japan's economic society has now entered a "post-catching-up" maturing stage. As a result, population growth is heading for stability, economic growth is shifting to medium speed, and Japan's international position and responsibility are becoming strongly recognized.

If Japan's development is likened to the process of human growth, then Japan has passed through a period of youth with growth and absorption, and has now entered a manhood or mellowing stage with internal improvement.

## 2. Limits to Conventional Thinking

At such a turning point, it is not proper to adhere to conventional thinking, systems and practices. They should be reexamined from a fresh point of view.

["Catching-Up-Type" Ideas]
First, there is no longer any room for the "cathing-up-type" way of thinking which seeks models of industrial structure, technological innovation and national life in developed Western nations, and positively introduces them into Japan to promote the progress of the nation.

Thus far, the history of Japan's development has been a history of change to an economic society of the Western type. Nonetheless, now that Japan has economically reached the level of developed nations and that socially, the troubles of the West European-type welfare society are becoming clear, an economic society of the Western type can no longer be a model for Japan.

From now on, Japan must open up a path of its own both economically and socially.

[Settlement of Problems Mainly Through Growth]

Second, it is no longer possible to resolve various problems of an economic society through high growth.

During the period of high growth, policy goals such as full employment and better welfare were achieved with relative ease by enlarging the "pie" through growth. Henceforth, it will become necessary to give full play to the vitality of the Japanese economy amid medium growth and deal with various policy problems from a fresh point of view.

["Small Nation" Theory No Longer Warranted]

Third, it is no longer permissible for Japan to behave on the basis of the "small-nation theory," which pays no heed to the possible impact of its conduct upon other countries.

When Japan's weight in the world economy was still small, it took the rest of the world for granted. But now that its economic position has increased, Japan has reached a stage in which it must deport itself with full awareness of the possible impact on the world economy.

To date, Japan has achieved efficient development with favorable international factors as a given condition for the relatively clear purpose of overtaking the developed nations in the West. However, with such a "catching-up" process now over, Japan is, in a way, deprived of a goal. From now on, Japan must tread a creative path that will take full advantage of its strong and advantageous points without simply imitating the path that other nations have already walked.

## 3. New "Grand Design"

[An Important 20 Years Ahead]

The next 20 years — the subject of this study — are considered to have important significance in various ways.

First, Japan will have to resolve a host of problems in a different way from the past amid the changing economic society.

On the other hand, as for the vitality of the economy which ought to form the basis for the settlement of such problems, it appears possible to continue medium growth for at least 20 years by maintaining such vitality.

Since the end of the war, Japan has achieved economic prosperity with few parallels in the world. However, at a time when Japan's economic society is facing a major turning point, it is becoming gradually more difficult to pursue the same path as in the past. It is thus becoming essential to build systems befitting a new age, stocks of good quality and amicable international relations, and to hand them over to posterity. If such both tangible and intangible assets are not built, Japan's economic society will face tremendous difficulties. Whether the postwar economic prosperity will take on historical significance or not will hinge upon whether in the next 20 years we can leave behind such tangible and intangible assets for the future by bringing our vitality into full play.

[A Favorable Time]
In considering these matters, Japan now finds itself under relatively favorable conditions.

First, the diverse changes expected in the 21st century have yet to take full shape. Thus, Japan still has time to take proper countermeasures.

Japan's population, economic society and international environment are faced with major changes with the approach of the 21st century, and Japan will have to settle various problems amid such changes. Nevertheless, 20 years may be called a period long enough to take various steps, including institutional reform, in coping with various long-term problems strategically.

Second, regarding the various problems found in a mature society, Japan can learn lessons from the experiences of Western society which treads the path first.

At present, Japan has just entered a maturing stage, but Western countries have been experiencing such a stage for a considerable time now, suffering from such difficulties as a decline in vitality. Japan can build a dynamic, mature society by taking such experiences into consideration.

Third, when viewed from the angle of technological innovation, Japan now measures up to the world's top level in electronics-related technologies which have vast potential. It will thus be possible to have technological innovation in such fields be conducive to Japan's economic development, international contribution and adjustment to the change in the economic society.

Hereafter, Japan should make full use of these favorable conditions and, determine correctly the course of the economic society in long-term perspective.

[Necessity of a "Grand Design"]

The above being the case, it is now necessary to have a new "grand design" looking into the 21st century.

The word "grand" used here has the following meanings.

First, it means "thinking in long-term perspective." In order to foresee long-term problems in the period until the 21st century, it is essential to have long-term perspective based on historical perception, without being preoccupied with short-term trends.

Second, it means "thinking about the economic society as a whole from a broad point of view." Over the long term, the economy and society will continue to change while affecting each other. When considering long-term problems, it is imperative to have a broad field of vision.

Third, the word signifies "showing a basic direction, and thinking without being wedded to details." When we consider uncertainties and an increasingly diversified sense of values in the fairly long period until the 21st century, the long-term design should be a pliable and flexible one.

[Outline of "Grand Design"]

On the basis of the above way of thinking, we shall present a "grand design" looking toward the 21st century, constituting the following chapters. Its rough outline is as follows:

Chapter 2 "Basic Prospects for the 21st Century" will give a rough sketch of the international environment, the state of the domestic economic society, and the expected changes in the period under review, which will be necessary for our long-term outlook.

Chapter 3 "Three Trends and a Basic Strategy for the 21st Century" will show the characteristic direction of the change in Japan's economic society and clarify the basic strategy for coping with various problems that will crop up in the process of such a change.

# Chapter 2    Basic Prospects for the 21st Century

    This chapter will provide a fundamental concept of the framework of the international environment and of the Japanese economic society over the period leading to the 21st century.

    To give our readers a clearer picture of how these will change over the coming years, we will attempt to represent them in quantitative terms as much as possible. However, there is a limit to such an approach especially when the period to be reviewed is as long as 20 years. It may be dangerous to attach too much importance to the figures given in this study. The quantitative framework in this chapter is provided simply to make the nature of possible changes easier to understand. Therefore, the figures ought to be interpreted with much latitude.

## Section 1    Image of the International Environment

### 1.    Basic Concept of the World Economy

    The world economy after World War II generally made smooth headway throughout the 1950s and 1960s, supported by the development of international mutual dependence. In the 1970s, however, it entered a phase of turmoil and uncertainty as it experienced the collapse of the Bretton Woods monetary agreement, two global oil crises and stagflation in most industrialized economies.

[How the 1980s and 1990s Should Be Viewed]
    The 1980s may be viewed as a decade of adjustment in which the world economy tries to pull out of turmoil and gropes towards a new order. If the world economy can successfully cope with these tasks in the 1980s, then it will be able to regain its vigor in the 1990s.

    We will now look at long-term trends for the world economy and some of the major tasks it faces there, and give our basic cognizance of these five problem areas — (1) the progress of multipolarization, (2) changes in international mutual dependence, (3) the decline in vitality of the world economy, (4) unstable energy and food situations, and (5) global population and environmental problems.

## (1) The Progress of Multipolarization

[Multipolarization in Both Eastern and Western Blocs]
    The world economy has been showing a trend toward multipolarization both in the free countries of the West and the socialist countries of the East.
    After World War II, Western countries developed under the lead of the powerful U.S. economy. The United States carried out the Marshall Plan to help postwar rehabilitation of Western Europe and strived to maintain the international economic order primarily built around the IMF and GATT. In the meantime, Western Europe and Japan have grown relatively stronger with the resultant decline in the power of the United States. Today the United States, Europe and Japan form a triangle that encompasses the world's industrialized democracies.
    Among the Socialist countries, East European countries have sought to promote their economic development through closer relations of mutual dependence with Western countries. And China has now shifted from its traditional policy of self-reliance and is getting ready to strengthen its relations with industrialized Western countries in order to promote its economic development.

[Differentiating Between Developing Countries]
    Throughout the 1950s and 1960s, the industrialized countries of the North and the developing countries of the South remained as two distinctively separate groups. In recent years, however, an economic differential has begun to surface among the Southern countries. One of the factors behind this is the rise in economic power of the OPEC countries. Their income levels have improved dramatically since a series of oil price increases after 1973. OPEC is now a major power that influences the world economy.
    Another factor is the rise of the newly industrializing countries (NICs). South Korea, Hong Kong, Singapore, Brazil and Mexico, for example, have succeeded in accelerating their economic growth through industrialization. Some of them now expect to graduate from the school of developing countries.

[The Process Leading to Stabilized Multipolarization]

This multipolarization of the world economy is seen as certain to continue. The gaps in economic power between the industrialized countries will continue to narrow. Even if the United States succeeds in revitalizing its economy, it will hardly regain the status of superpower that it enjoyed in the 1960s. Nor will other countries including Japan be able to assume outright hegemony.

Meanwhile, the newly industrialized countries, will continue to attain relatively high economic growth, rapidly catching up with industrialized countries. Some of the developing countries in the medium income bracket will also try to catch up with some of the industrialized and newly industrializing countries.

During the 20-year period leading to the 21st Century, the world economy will undergo a process of groping for stability under this multipolarization.

(2) Changes in Mutual Dependence

[Economic Development amid Progress in Mutual Dependence]

One great feature characterizing world economic undercurrents in postwar years is that economic development has been ensured and promoted through the progress in mutual economic dependence between countries or groups of countries.

The ratio of world export value to world GNP (in real terms) rose constantly from 7.4% in 1960 to 9.7% in 1970 and 11.5% in 1980 (See Table 2-1-1). This indicates the closeness with which international mutual dependence between countries has progressed over the years. This closer international mutual dependence has prompted the international division of labor, and made sure of efficient economic activity on a global basis.

[What Prompted Mutual Dependence?]

Mutual dependence has progressed not only in international trade but in many other areas like capital movement, personnel interchange and cultural exchange. Several factors have contributed to this.

The first is the progress in transportation and communication facilities, which has made the countries of the world less remote and more uniform.

**Table 2-1-1 Changes in World Trade (in real terms)**

(In $1 billion at 1970 price)

| Year | 1960 | 1965 | 1970 | 1975 | 1980 |
|---|---|---|---|---|---|
| (A) World GNP | 1,975 | 2,543 | 3,250 | 3,929 | 4,679 |
| (B) World exports (on an FOB basis) | 146 | 205 | 314 | 404 | 536 |
| Ratio of world exports to world GNP (B)/(A) | 7.4% | 8.1% | 9.7% | 10.3% | 11.5% |

**Note:** The Figures have been prepared by the Planning Bureau of the Economic Planning Agency. World GNP figures are based on the U.S. Government publication, "The Soviet Economy under Transformation" (October 1979) and the "Economic Report of the President." World export figures are based on the U.N. publications, "Yearbook of International Trade Statistics" and "Monthly Bulletin of Statistics."

A second contributing factor is the organization of a global framework to enhance trade and capital liberalization. Under the leadership of the United States, two basic frameworks — the IMF for monetary and financial markets and GATT for international trade — have been firmly upheld. These have played an important role in developing the world economy under the principles of freedom, non-discrimination and multilateralism.

A third factor is the increasingly bigger role played by those who have acted in accordance with principles transcending national boundaries, as exemplified by the development of international financial and capital markets and the growing activities of multinational business corporations. These have made national boundaries a nominal existence and strengthened international economic relations.

[Changes in Mutual Dependence]

However, since the turn of the 1970s, it has become increasingly difficult to maintain such stable international mutual dependence.

The international monetary system, based on the IMF, used to rely on the United States' balance of payments deficit for the supply of much of its necessary liquidity. But the confidence in the value of the dollar was shaken by the relative decline in the economic power of the United States. The world's major countries had to switch to the floating exchange scheme in 1973 following the so-called Nixon shock of 1971 when the dollar's convertibility was suspended.

The 1973 oil crisis also gave rise to new problems such as the recycling of oil money accumulated in the OPEC countries and the rescheduling of debts amassed in non-oil producing developing countries.

In the 1970s, even within the free trade system under the aegis of GATT, the United States and Western Europe began to face increasing imports caused by the decline in their competitive edge and difficulties in adjusting their domestic industry, and repeatedly moved to restrict imports with the resultant recurrence of economic friction with their trading partners. Developing countries with abundant natural resources now have a much bigger say and tend to pursue a policy of preserving their resources, particularly oil.

The progress of mutual dependence indeed promotes international division of labor and contributes a great deal toward the development of the world economy as a whole. On the other hand, however, it makes the economic performance of individual countries more vulnerable to external factors. Problems they are apt to face include economic confusion caused by drastic increases in oil prices, the adjustment of macro-economic policies necessitated by the international influence of business cycles and violent fluctuations in exchange rates, and the adjustment of domestic industry and trade friction.

[The Future for Mutual Dependence]

Fundamentally, international, economic mutual dependence is expected to develop in the future. For one thing, individual economies are already deeply incorporated into a network of international mutual dependence. Strongly established economic relations will not fall back so easily.

With continued international efforts, stable mutual dependence may well be developed further to the benefit of the world economy.

## (3)  Decline in the Vitality of the World Economy

[Postwar Development of the World Economy]

The world economy grew at a fairly rapid pace in postwar years. This was made possible because the governments of industrialized countries pursued positive economic policies primarily aimed at attaining full employment, the free trade system was upheld under the aegis of both the IMF and GATT, and countries could enjoy growing consumer demand centered on durable consumer goods.

Technological innovations have also played a major role in accelerating economic growth. The postwar development of new technologies in both heavy and chemical industries and the electric appliance industry has helped to lead the economic growth of industrialized countries and the world as a whole by improving labor productivity through mass production and creating new demands. A new wave of technological innovations involving computers, electronic instruments and integrated circuits is now gathering momentum across the world.

[The Decline in Vitality in Recent Years]

In recent years, however, the world economy has apparently been losing its vitality since it has experienced two major oil crises.

The industrialized economies of the United States and Western Europe have been continuing to struggle with stagflation that began after the first oil crisis.

Non-oil producing countries, too, suffer from worsening balance of payments problems and snowballing external debts, badly hit by higher oil prices and the economic slump in industrialized countries. Socialist countries are no exception. There, economic growth tends to be slow due to the slump in agriculture and industry. Thus economic activity remains depressed and international trade dull across the world.

[The Disease Suffered by Industrialized Countries]

If one sees the trends in industrialized countries from a slightly long-term standpoint, it is clear that most of them suffer what may be called an advanced nations' disease characterized by such symptoms as increasing absenteeism, growing bureaucracy and a decline in enthusiasm for investment, which often lead to deceleration in the improvement of labor productivity, continuation of stagflation and other examples of poor economic performance.

These trends have prompted many of these countries to reconsider the role played by the government and take steps to reinvigorate the economy on the supply side, including those aimed at stirring up business enthusiasm to invest.

[Difficulties in a Zero-Sum Situation]
Such a decline in vitality of the world economy tends to slow down the growth of national economies and creates a so-called "zero-sum" situation, bringing to the surface a number of difficulties with which the world economy is then confronted.

In such a situation, adjustment of the industrial structure is harder to make. The employment situation becomes serious, inviting occasional calls for protectionism, thus making it increasingly difficult to maintain the free trade system.

(4)  Unstable Energy and Food Situations

[The Gap in Energy Supplies]
While the world energy situation remained relatively stable in 1981 and 1982, the longer-term prospects are far from secure.

It will not be until after the turn of the next century that synthesized fuel and other new energy sources come into the market in abundance. Conventional alternative energy sources such as nuclear power, coal and natural gas will claim increasingly larger shares in total energy supplies. But much time will be needed before these energy sources can be fully developed and put to commercial use. Markets for such alternative energy sources competitive enough to brake a rise in oil prices are not expected to be formed and developed before the middle of the 1990s.

The period leading to the 21st century, specifically the first 10 years, will see a "gap in energy supplies" that continues as oil is replaced by other energy sources. Throughout this period the world economy will remain insecure at the mercy of OPEC's oil policies. Japan, which is highly dependent on imported oil, will remain exposed to a potential threat.

[Prospects for World Energy Supply and Demand]

Table 2-1-2 gives the Free World's prospective energy supply and demand in the year 2000. The estimates have been drawn from the actual volumes of oil supply and demand in recent years, progress in anergy-saving efforts and projects underway for the development of alternative energy sources.

Future energy supply and demand will differ depending on OPEC's price policies and the growth of the economies of individual countries. Assuming that the Free World's economic growth will average 3% annually, that energy consumption per unit of GNP (which indicates how energy consumption is saved) will decline gradually and that the effective price of oil will increase 2% a year on the average, the total energy demand in the year 2000 will be about 1.6 times the level in 1980.

Supply and demand will balance if crude oil production and the synthesized fuel supply turn out to be at the top end of the estimates. However, there will be a gap if the OPEC oil production is kept at some 25 million barrels per day or the synthesized fuel supply turns out to be at the bottom end of the estimates. In the latter case, the Free World will inevitably face a difficult situation.

[World Food Supply and Demand in Recent Years]

Basically the world enjoyed an oversupply of grains until 1972, when the situation changed dramatically because of poor farm crops due to unusual climatic changes and the massive grain purchases by the Soviet Union. The world's grain supplies have remained insecure ever since.

The following points ought to be noted in discussing long-term food supply and demand.

(1)  Grain production tends to fluctuate violently according to changes in weather conditions, as the arable land available gradually expands into less arable areas.

(2)  Amid increasing demand caused mainly by the population growth in developing countries, there is a widening gap in food consumption standards between the rich North and poor South.

(3)  Demand for feed grain is increasing as an improvement in standards of living encourages more consumption of livestock products.

(4)  Increased grain imports by the Soviet Union and China and

## Table 2-1-2 The Outlook for the World (Free World) Primary Energy Supply-Demand Balance

| Year | 1980 | 2000 | |
|---|---|---|---|
| Case | Actual supply and demand | Case 1 | Case 2 |
| **Average annual economic growth rate between 1980 and 2000 (%)** | | | |
| Industrialized nations | | 2.0 | 2.5 |
| Developing nations | | 4.2 | 4.8 |
| Average of free world nations | | 2.5 | 3.0 |
| **Total primary energy demand (in million B/D)** | | | |
| Industrialized nations | 77.3 | 99 | 109 |
| Developing nations | 19.4 | 41.2 | 45.4 |
| (1) Total of free world nations | 96.7 | 140.2 | 154.6 |

| Items / Energy | 1980 Volume of supply in terms of oil (in million B/D) | 1980 Percentage share (%) | Case 1 Volume of supply in terms of oil (in million B/D) | Case 2 Volume of supply in terms of oil (in million B/D) | Percentage share (%) |
|---|---|---|---|---|---|
| Nuclear power | 3.0 | 3.1 | 15.7 | 15.7 | 11.0~10.1 |
| Coal | 20.1 | 20.8 | 36.5 | 36.5 | 25.5~23.6 |
| Natural gas | 17.5 | 18.1 | 26.7 | 26.7 | 18.7~17.2 |
| Hydroelectric power and others | 7.1 | 7.3 | 13.1 | 13.1 | 9.2~8.5 |
| Total | 47.7 | 49.3 | 92.0 | 92.0 | 64.4~59.4 |
| OPEC Crude oil | 26.8 | 27.7 | 23.4~29.5 | 16.4~19.0 | |
| Non-OPEC crude oil etc. | 22.2 | 23.0 | 22.5~26.5 | 15.7~17.1 | |
| Synthetic fuel oil | — | — | 5.0~7.0 | 3.5~4.5 | |
| Total | 49.0 | 50.7 | 50.9~63.0 | 35.6~40.6 | |
| (2) Sum total | 96.7 | 100 | 142.9~155.0 | 100 | |
| Supply-Demand gap (2) – (1) | — | — | 2.7~14.8 | −11.7~0.4 | |

Notes:

1. **Sources:** Compiled from BP Statistics and data supplied by the Japan Research Institute of Energy Economics.
2. Crude oil supply is equivalent to crude oil output.
3. Non-OPEC crude oil etc. includes NGL.

an expanded U.S. share in exports have brought about regional imbalances of supply and demand, which in turn are causing the world grain trade structure to change.

(5)  Food has come to be used politically and diplomatically after the United States announced an embargo on grain exports in 1980 as part of its sanctions against the Soviet Union.

[Future Prospects]

The world food supply and demand in the years 2000 are estimated in Table 2-1-3. Population growth in developing countries may lead to a major increase in food demand. But supply will be able to meet demand in view of an increase in the production per unit of acreage.

But the following problems remain.

In the first place, the present pattern of industrialized countries meeting the growing food shortage of Socialist countries and developing countries will become increasingly evident, and the regional imbalances in food supply and demand will widen further.

Secondly, because of population growth, increased grain production and imports by developing countries will not lead to any substantial increase in per-capita food consumption. The North-South gap in food consumption will continue to widen.

Thirdly, because of a limit to the expansion of farmable land, future efforts for increased grain production will be concentrated on boosting the output per unit of acreage. This will result in increased production costs which in turn will push grain prices upward over a long period of time.

Fourthly, because greater efforts will be made to cultivate marginal land and make intensive use of cultivated land, grain production fluctuation due to changes in weather conditions will become more frequent and prominent.

Fifthly, with grain supplies limited virtually to the United States and a handful of other countries, the world will have to tolerate a seller's market to an increasing extent.

All these seem to point to a continued instability in world food supply and demand over the coming years.

**Table 2-1-3 The Outlook for World Grain Demand and Supply**

| | Base year | | | 2000 | | | Contribution of population increase to consumption increase (between base year and the year 2000) (%) |
|---|---|---|---|---|---|---|---|
| | Production (million tons) | Per-capita consumption (kg) | Demand-supply gap (million tons) | Production (million tons) | Per-capita consumption (kg) | Demand-supply gap (million tons) | |
| MAFF estimate (1982) | | | | | | | |
| World | 1,409 | 327 | — | 2,171 | 341 | — | 70 |
| Advanced nations | 508 | 556 | +79 | 735 | 659 | +156 | 41 |
| Socialist nations | 529 | 410 | -41 | 763 | 450 | -77 | 71 |
| Developing nations | 372 | 191 | -34 | 673 | 208 | -79 | 82 |
| U.S. estimate (1980) | | | | | | | |
| World | 1,203 | 313 | — | 2,197~2,142 | 352~343 | — | 54 |
| Advanced nations | 435 | 511 | +62 | 740~679 | 735~692 | +91~+68 | 21 |
| Socialist nations | 439 | 396 | -24 | 722 | 474 | -37 | 61 |
| Developing nations | 329 | 182 | -30 | 735~741 | 210~206 | -55~-32 | 70 |
| FAO estimate (1981) | | | | | | | |
| Developing nations | 382 | 196 | -33 | 696 | 221 | -105 | 77 |

**Notes:**

1. **Sources:** Ministry of Agriculture, Forestry and Fisheries (MAFF) "The Estimate of Food Supply and Demand Based on the World Food Supply-Demand Model"; U.S. Government "The Global 2000 Report to the President"; FAO "The Outlook for Agriculture in the year 2000."

2. Both MAFF and U.S. estimates are based on "Case 1," while the FAO estimate is based on "Scenario B."

3. The base year is the average between 1977 and 1979 in the MAFF estimate, the average between 1973 and 1975 in the U.S. estimate, and the average between 1975 and 1979 in the FAO estimate.

4. The definition of socialist countries and developing countries differs according to each agency.

(5)   Global Population and Environmental Problems

[Population Growth Mainly in Developing Countries]
The world's population has increased markedly since the end of World War II. The total rose to 4,434 million in 1980 from 2,500 million in 1950. Much of the growth was due to a significant fall in the mortality rate and a still high level in the birth rate, mainly in developing countries.

The growth of population is expected to slow down in future in both industrialized and developing countries. But the world's population will reach somewhere around 6,200 to 6,300 million in the year 2000 (See Table 2-1-4). Roughly 90% of the population increase over the coming years will be in developing countries, particularly the least developed countries. The proportion of the developing world's population to the total world population will rise accordingly to some 80% in the year 2000 from some 70% in 1960 and 75% in 1980.

This population explosion in developing countries will aggravate the North-South problem, the food supply and demand situation and the migration problem.

[Global Environmental Problems]
Environmental problems on a global basis will assume greater importance in the future. Some of the problems already pointed out include:

(1)   The constant rise in the density of carbon dioxide ($CO_2$) in the atmosphere due to increased use of fossil fuels and a decrease in the earth's forests. According to a U.S. Government publication "The Global 2000 Report to the President" (1980), the density of carbon dioxide will double as compared with the present level in the year 2050, possibly raising the atmospheric temperature to an appreciable extent.

(2)   Desertification as a result of the disorderly use of land and excessive grazing will increase. The same publication predicts that the earth's total desert area will increase to one billion hectares in the year 2000 from the present 800 million hectares.

(3)   The possible extinction of some animal and plant species due to ecological destruction. It is said that some 130 wild bird and mammal species have become extinct since 1600.

**Table 2-1-4  Estimate of World Population**

| Year | 1980 U.N. estimate | | | The Global 2000 Report to the President | | | Interfutures |
|---|---|---|---|---|---|---|---|
| | World | Advanced nations | Developing nations | World | Advanced nations | Developing nations | World |
| 1950 | 2,525 | 832 | 1,693 | | | | |
| 1955 | 2,757 | 887 | 1,870 | | | | |
| 1960 | 3,037 | 945 | 2,092 | | | | |
| 1965 | 3,354 | 1,003 | 2,351 | | | | |
| 1970 | 3,696 | 1,047 | 2,648 | | | | |
| 1975 | 4,067 | 1,092 | 2,975 | 4,090 | 1,131 | 2,959 | 3,970 |
| 1980(A) | 4,434 | 1,131 | 3,303 | 4,470 | 1,170 | 3,301 | 4,370 |
| 1985 | 4,828 | 1,170 | 3,658 | 4,885 | 1,212 | 3,673 | 4,820 |
| 1990 | 5,244 | 1,206 | 4,038 | 5,340 | 1,252 | 4,088 | 5,280 |
| 1995 | 5,679 | 1,242 | 4,437 | 5,834 | 1,290 | 4,544 | 5,760 |
| 2000(B) | 6,121 | 1,272 | 4,849 | 6,351 | 1,323 | 5,028 | 6,250 |
| (B)−(A) | 1,687 | 141 | 1,546 | 1,881 | 153 | 1,727 | 1,880 |

Notes:
1. **Sources:**  U.N. "Estimate of Population" (1980); U.S. Government "The Global 2000 Report to the President"; OECD "Interfutures."
2. Advanced nations, as defined by the U.S., comprise Europe, North America, Japan, Australia, New Zealand and the Soviet Union.
3. Advanced nations, as defined by "The Global 2000 Report to the President," include temperate South American countries as well (Argentina, Chile, Faulkland Islands and Uruguay).
4. All are based on medium variant.

The IUCN (International Union for Conservation of Nature and Natural Resources) believes that as many as 674 species of vertebrate animals are now on the verge of extinction due mainly to destruction of their habitats.

These environmental problems have not been fully identified and appreciated. However, the environment, once lost, can hardly be restored fully. Mankind could lose out on the earth's still unknown great potentialities. In the future, Japan must join the rest of the world in conserving the environment as mankind's common asset.

## 2. Outlook for the World Economy

### (1) Main Factors Affecting World Economic Trends

Predictions may differ as to how the world economy will fare over the period leading up to the 21st century, but basic future trends will be determined by these factors.

[Trends for Mutually Dependent Relationships]

The first factor will be how mutual international economic relations change over the coming years. If the present shaky world economic system can be mended and international collaboration maintained and strengthened, the world economy and trade will continue to enjoy sustained growth, and the Japanese economy will go on developing under stable international conditions.

However, if stable international mutual relations cannot be maintained, tensions will build up, impairing the growth of the world economy and trade. Japan will then have to face a number of difficulties.

[Growth Potential of Industrialized Countries]

The second factor relates to the growth potential of industrialized economies. If revolutionary technological developments are achieved in these countries and a loss of vitality, peculiar to the "advanced country disease," can be prevented, their growth potential will be fully displayed and Japan will also be able to maintain good economic performance.

On the other hand, if technological innovation declines and the various symptoms of the "advanced country disease" cannot be cured, the economic growth of industrialized countries will inevitably slow down. Japan, too, will be hardly able to maintain its economic vitality.

[Trends for the World Energy Situation and Reaction of Consumer Countries]

The third factor involved is how the world energy situation will change and how consumer countries will react. If oil supplies become stable and if consumer countries make progress both in the development of alternative energy sources and energy conservation, energy will not be a serious problem for either the world economy on the Japanese economy.

However, if the Middle East situation turns worse and if little progress is made by consumer countries in the development of alternative energy sources, actual oil prices will rise substantially, aggravating the economic performances of industrialized countries. Japan will be affected more seriously because of its high dependence on imported oil.

(2) Assumptions in Drawing Up a Long-Term Outlook

Views on future prospect for the world economy may differ depending on how these factors are assessed. There are many uncertain factors that may affect the future prospects for international politics and the world economy. Given the difficult situation now confronting the world, any wrong approach could bring about a prolonged slump or even a catastrophe to the world economy. As such a situation will bring out a confused and insecure situation all over the world, it must be avoided by all means. The immediate priority for Japan is to step up solidarity and collaboration with the rest of the world to prevent such a confused and insecure situation. In drawing up a long-term outlook, it may be worth while assuming such a pessimistic situation. But this Committee will not adopt such an approach, for to do so may give rise to misunderstanding about our view of the world situation or obscure our point of view. We will base our work on the assumption that, as we will see in Chapter 3, both Japan and other countries of the world will adopt the best conceivable policies for addressing the difficult problems they face. Other assumptions on which we will base our work are as follows:

[Fundamental Future Course of the World Economy]

In international economic relations, we assume that the world economy will continue to grow as the free trade system is basically maintained and mutual international relations are gradually promoted. But because friction resulting from industrial adjustment may become tense occasionally, we don't expect the same stable framework of international economic relations as we saw in the 1960s.

We assume that stagflation will not be easy to overcome and that the growth in industrialized countries over the coming years will be somewhat slower than in the 1960s and 1970s, even if some progress is made in their efforts for industrial revitalization.

We do not premise that the world economy will be jolted by a dramatic increase in oil prices as on the occasion of the first and second oil crises, for we look forward to some progress in international collaboration between consumer countries for the development of alternative energy sources, conservation of energy and the stockpiling of oil. However, we assume that actual oil prices will go on climbing moderately, as energy conservation efforts by consuming countries will become less serious, the OPEC countries will not change their policy of adjusting crude oil production, and the political situation in the Middle East will remain basically unstable.

[Regional Outlook]

Based on our assumptions regarding the world economy, we visualize the growth patterns in major regional economies over the last two decades of the 20th century as follows:

(1) The U.S. and European industrialized economies will gradually recover from recession, but their annual growth rate will be somewhat lower at around 2½% compared with 3% or so in the 1970s.

(2) Among the developing countries, newly industrializing countries are likely to register growth considerably higher than in industrialized countries. We assume an annual growth rate of around 6%.

(3) The annual growth rate in other developing countries will be somewhere around 4%. We assume that oil producing countries will

find it harder to raise their income levels through major oil price increases, that some non-oil producing countries in the medium income bracket will begin to match newly industrializing countries in economic growth, and that developing countries in the low income (Southern Asian countries and African countries south of the Sahara) bracket will continue to experience slow growth, due to population, food and balance of payments difficulties.

(4) It is harder, under limited conditions, to predict the growth prospects for Socialist countries, where a number of factors are unstable. Moderate growth can be expected for some Eastern European countries. However, in view of the poor performances of both agriculture and industry in recent years and because of the likelihood that some of the present economic difficulties will remain unsolved, we assume that the average growth rate in the Soviet Union and its European allies will be around 3% against an average 5% in the 1970s. However, the growth rate in China will be a little higher at 4% or so as the Chinese alter their policies in favor of closer economic relations with Western countries.

(3) Japan's Growth Outlook

[Change in World GNP Composition]
Prospective regional and national shares in world GNP in the year 2000 are given in Table 2-1-5. These are based on both the premises mentioned above and on the assumption that Japan will continue to post faster economic growth than other industrialized countries as mentioned in Section 2 in this chapter.

It is clear from the Table that the United States, accounting for a large proportion of the world GNP, will remain a major economic power in the year 2000. Along with Japan and the European Community, it will be one of the world's three major economic blocs. However, the weight of the industrialized economies as a whole will decline in the year 2000 in contrast with a greater proportion to be assumed by the developing countries, particularly the newly industrializing countries.

Even if the Japanese economy should grow faster than the economies of other advanced countries, its growth rate would prove slower than that of the developing countries. Japan's share in world

## Table 2-1-5　World GNP Composition in 2000

(In %)

| | GNP composition in 1960 | Present GNP composition | Real economic growth rate (annual rate) Latest 10 years (1970-1979) | Real economic growth rate (annual rate) 1980-2000 | GNP composition in 2000 |
|---|---|---|---|---|---|
| **Industrialized countries** | | | | | |
| Japan | 3 | 10 | 5.2 | 4.0 | 12 |
| U.S. | 33 | 22 | 3.1 | 2.5 | 20 |
| EC and other OECD members | 26 | 31 | 3.1 | | 26 |
| Total | (62) | (63) | (3.3) | (2.8) | (58) |
| **Developing countries** | | | | | |
| Newly industrializing countries | 3 | 4 | 8.0 | 6.0 | 7 |
| Other LDC's | 11 | 11 | 5.7 | 4.0 | 13 |
| Total | (14) | (15) | (6.3) | (4.6) | (20) |
| **Socialist countries** | | | | | |
| USSR | 15 | 13 | 5.1 | 3.0 | 12 |
| East Europe, etc. | 4 | 5 | 5.9 | | 5 |
| China | 5 | 5 | 5.8 | 4.0 | 5 |
| Total | (24) | (22) | (5.4) | (3.2) | (22) |
| World total | 100 | 100 | 4.3 | 3.2 | 100 |

**Notes:**

1. The economic growth rates were estimated by the Planning Bureau of the Economic Planning Agency on the basis of the world economic outlook given in this study.
2. The present GNP composition is at 1978 prices (in U.S. dollars).
3. Newly industrializing countries are South Korea, Hong Kong, Singapore, Brazil, Mexico and Taiwan.

GNP may continue to expand, but not as fast as in the past. We assume that Japan's share in the year 2000 will be around 12%, compared with 10% at present.

However, Japan's share in the combined GNP of industrialized countries will grow faster to reach 21% in the year 2000 from the present 16%.

Developing countries may enjoy faster growth. But because of rapid population growth, per-capita income in these countries (other than the newly industrializing countries) will not increase proportionately. Therefore, they will continue to suffer a major income gap compared with industrialized countries, including Japan.


[World Economic Map in Year 2000]

These prospective changes in regional economic power have been transposed into the world economic maps in Figure 2-1-6 (in which the size of national GNP has been translated proportionately into area).

Reduction of the U.S. area and expansion of the Japanese and European areas are clear from a comparison of the 1960 map and the present map. Over the next 20 years, the U.S. area will continue to shrink, while the areas of Japan and other Asian countries will go on expanding.

The changes may not be as drastic as in the past 20 years. Yet they will be of major significance to Japan, for they imply that many of the neighboring countries will develop much faster over the years leading up to the 21st century.


[Outlook for World Trade]

The Prospective shares of the industrialized countries, developing countries and Socialist countries in total world trade are given in Table 2-1-7. The figures are based on economic growth estimates. This table indicates that both the trade between industrialized countries and exports from developing countries to industrialized countries will assume greater proportions in future. This will happen because the economies of developing countries are likely to grow relatively faster and because developing countries will export more industrial products to advanced countries as they make progress in industrialization.

Faster economic growth in developing countries and an expansion

## Fig. 2-1-6　World Economic Map

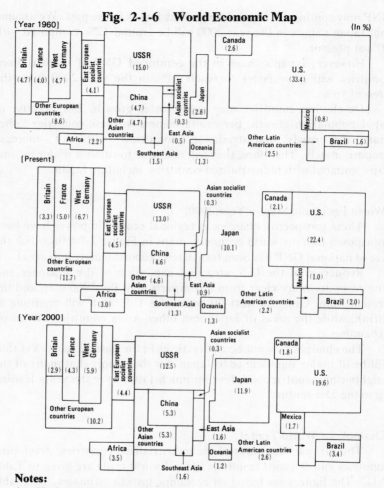

**Notes:**
1. National GNP shares in the year 2000 are based on the figures given in Table 2-1-5.
2. The map are based on the assumption that the GNP growth rate of a group of countries is identical to that of each country. It is inappropriate to attempt an international comparison of growth rates.
3. Figures in parentheses denote national or regional shares in world GNP.

## Table 2-1-7  The Outlook for Commodity Trade Matrix

Year 1980 (In %)

| Exports \ Imports | World | Industrialized countries | Developing countries | Socialist countries |
|---|---|---|---|---|
| World | 100 | 66 | 21 | 13 |
| Industrialized countries | 65 | 46 | 14 | 5 |
| Developing countries | 25 | 17 | 6 | 2 |
| Socialist countries | 11 | 4 | 1 | 6 |

Year 1990 (In %)

| Exports \ Imports | World | Industrialized countries | Developing countries | Socialist countries |
|---|---|---|---|---|
| World | 100 | 65 | 24 | 11 |
| Industrialized countries | 64 | 44 | 16 | 5 |
| Developing countries | 26 | 18 | 7 | 2 |
| Socialist countries | 10 | 4 | 2 | 5 |

Year 2000 (In %)

| Exports \ Imports | World | Industrialized countries | Developing countries | Socialist countries |
|---|---|---|---|---|
| World | 100 | 63 | 27 | 11 |
| Industrialized countries | 64 | 41 | 18 | 5 |
| Developing countries | 27 | 18 | 7 | 2 |
| Socialist countries | 9 | 4 | 2 | 4 |

**Note:** The figures were compiled by the Planning Bureau of the Economic Planning Agency from the UNCTAD "Handbook of International Trade and Development Statistics," U.N. "Yearbook of International Trade Statistics" and "Yearbook of National Accounts Statistics."

of mutual trade between these countries and industrialized countries will have great bearing on the future of world trade.

# Section 2　Outlook for the Japanese Economic Society

## 1.　Population, Households, Regions

### (1)　Population

The structure of a nation's population is determined by the birth rate, mortality rate and the volume of migration. Japan already boasts of its world-ranking longevity figures. The mortality rate may continue to fall in the long run, but any steep fall in the near future is not likely. Migration will remain insignificant. This leaves the birth rate as the most important factor to determine Japan's future population structure.

[Past Decline in Birth Rate]
Japan's birth rate dropped sharply after the postwar "baby boom" years and remained generally stable for the following 20 years. However, the birth rate began falling again in 1974 and the trend is still continuing. The recent decline in the birth rate may be attributed to (1) the decrease in the number of marriageable and child-bearing generations resulting from the post-baby boom fall in the birth rate, (2) girls seeking longer academic careers and marrying late, and (3) changes in economic conditions since the world oil crisis.

[Future Birth Rate]
The Institute of Population Problems of the Health and Welfare Ministry takes the view that Japan's birth rate, which declined in the latter half of the 1970s, will begin to recover before long. The institute points out that many of the girls born during the second "baby boom" in the first half of the 1970s will get married and reach maternity age. As the growing ratio of girls advancing to university or college starts leveling off, those who choose to marry late will decrease in number. The institute, noting that fewer people choose to remain single and that fewer couples in Japan decide not to have a child than in European countries, believes that the birth rate will recover once economic conditions are stabilized and people get accustomed to a new post-oil crisis lifestyle.

The institute also notes that the number of children an average

## Fig. 2-2-1  Actual Figures and Estimates of Total Fertility Rates

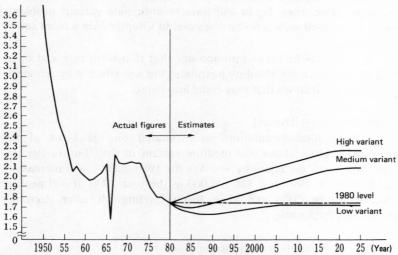

Actual figures | Estimates

High variant
Medium variant
1980 level
Low variant

1950 55 60 65 70 75 80 85 90 95 2000 5 10 15 20 25 (Year)

**Source:** Institute of Population Problems, Health and Welfare Ministry "Future Population Projections for Japan by Sex-Age for 1980-2080" (November 1981).

couple has as well as the number of children they expect to have additionally in future combined has been stable at an average 2.2 in recent years, and says that despite the recent fall in the birth rate, the number of children a couple may have during their marriage has basically not changed.

This study relies on the medium variant given in the "Future Population Projections for Japan by Sex-Age for 1980-2080" published in November 1981 by the Health and Welfare Ministry's Institute of Population Problems, and assumes that the total fertility rate (see footnote) will drop to 1.68 in 1985 from 1.74 in 1980 and then start rising moderately to reach 1.85 in the year 2000, and 2.09, the replacement level, in 2025 (See Figure 2-2-1).

(Note) The total fertility rate is the age-wise birth rates between 15 and 49 years of age put together. It gives the number of children a women will have in her lifetime, provided the age-wise birth rate at a certain year is maintained unchanged in future.

However, it must be noted that views differ widely about the future prospects for Japan's birth rate. If the birth rate does not recover as assumed above, then Japan will have to anticipate various problems posed by an aged society (to be discussed in Chapter 3) in a more severe perspective.

It must also be taken into account that that birth rate and other vital statistics are not absolute postulates but are affected by economic and social institutions that may come into being.

[Total Population Trends]

Japan's total population, as estimated on the basis of the assumption given above (the medium variant in the "Future Population Projections for Japan by Sex-Age for 1980-2080"), will increase to 122,830,000 in 1990 and 128,120,000 in the year 2000. It will peak at 130,360,000 in 2008 and then begin leveling off after declining moderately for a while.

[Changes in Population Composition]

The pattern of population pyramids will undergo prominent changes. In 1980, Japan's population pyramid looked like a bell with a sharp top. In the year 2000, when the "baby boom" generations move upwards, it will look like a pot. It will further change to a beer barrel-shaped pyramid in the year 2025 (See Figure 2-2-2).

In the meantime, the population balance will also change. The share of those aged 65 or over will rise to 15.6% in the year 2000 from 9.0% in 1980. One out of every 6.4 people in Japan will be aged 65 or over in the year 2000 compared with one out of every 11 people in 1985.

The balance between the productive population and the dependent population will also change. Normally, the productive population covers people aged between 15 and 64. But in this study, we cover those aged between 20 and 64, considering that almost all Japanese boys and girls advance to senior high school. We will call them the real productive population. With an increase in the number of people aged 65 or over counterbalanced by a drop in the number of the younger generation (those under 20), the real productive population will continue increasing until around the year 2000 (from 60.4% in 1980 to

# Fig. 2-2-2 Changes in the Population Pyramid

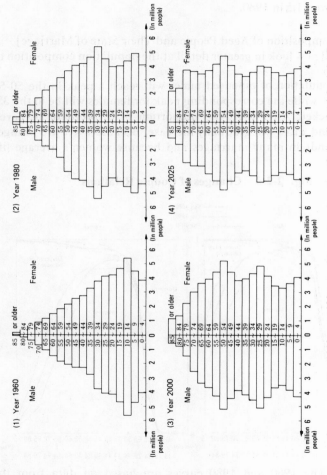

**Sources:** The 1960 and 1980 pyramids are based on the "Census" of the Statistics Bureau of the Prime Minister's Office. The 2000 and 2025 pyramids are based on the medium variant of the "Future Population Projections for Japan by Sex-Age for 1980-2080" (November 1981) of the Institute of Population Problems, the Health and Welfare Ministry.

61.3% in 2000). But it will begin to decrease abruptly thereafter, reaching 55.1% in the year 2015. Provided that the real productive population supports the economic life of other people, the number of people who must look after one other person will decrease to 1.2 in the year 2015 from 1.5 in 1980.

[The Sex Composition of Aged People and Their State of Marriage]
We will now look in greater detail at the population composition of aged people.

The population of espoused males will reach a peak in the 50-54 age bracket, while the corresponding peak for females will be in the 35-39 age bracket. After that, the proportion of divorced or bereaved husbands and wives will gradually increase. Because wives are younger than husbands in many marriages and because women's average life

## Fig. 2-2-3 Changes of Couple Relations

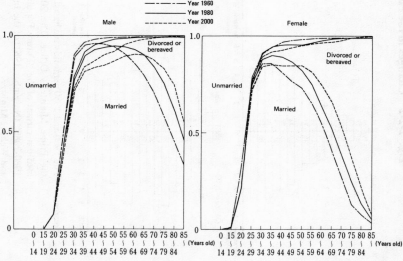

**Sources:** The 1960 and 1980 curves are based on data from the "Census" of the Statistics Bureau of the Prime Minister's Office, while the 2000 curve is based on the estimate by the Planning Bureau of the Economic Planning Agency.

## Fig. 2-2-4  Population by Age, Sex, Marital Status

(In 1,000 people)

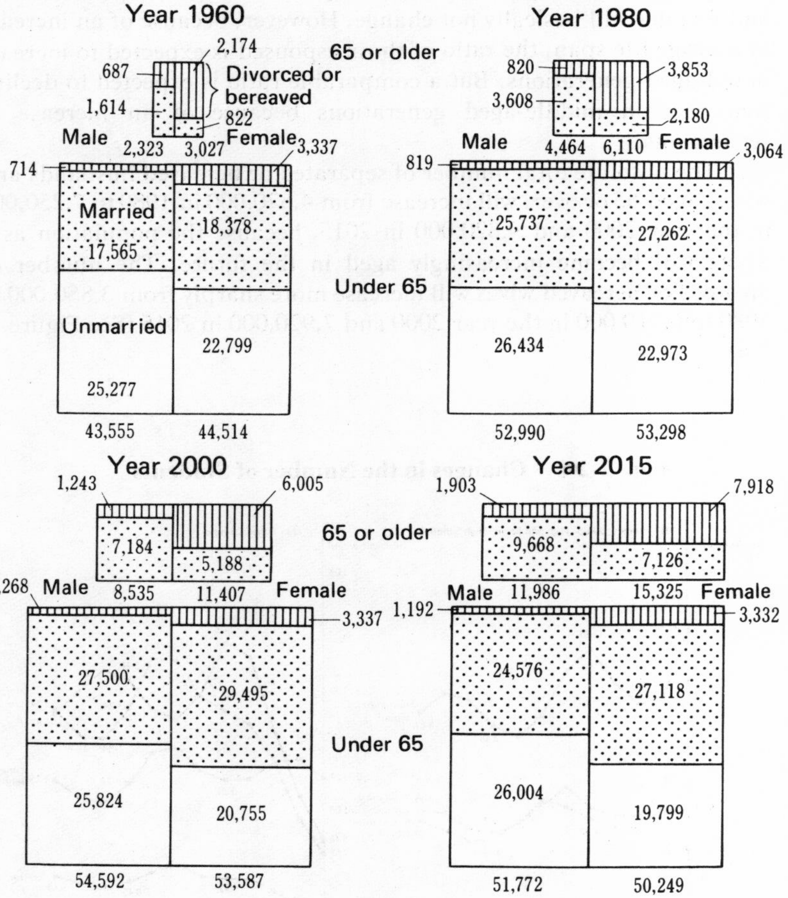

### Year 1960

```
                    2,174        65 or older
       687 ┐  ╱╱╱╱╱╱╱
           │  Divorced or
     1,614 ┤  bereaved
           │  822
Male  2,323  3,027  Female 3,337
714 ┐
    ┌─────────────┬──────────────┐
    │ Married     │   18,378     │
    │ 17,565      │              │
    ├─────────────┼──────────────┤
    │ Unmarried   │   22,799     │
    │             │              │ Under 65
    │ 25,277      │              │
    └─────────────┴──────────────┘
     43,555         44,514
```

### Year 1980

```
      820 ┐ ╱╱╱╱╱     3,853
          │
    3,608 ┤         2,180
Male  4,464  6,110  Female  3,064
819 ┐
    ┌─────────────┬──────────────┐
    │  25,737     │   27,262     │
    ├─────────────┼──────────────┤
    │             │              │
    │  26,434     │   22,973     │
    └─────────────┴──────────────┘
     52,990         53,298
```

### Year 2000

```
1,243 ┐              6,005
    ┌──────────┬─────────┐  65 or older
    │  7,184   │  5,188  │
    └──────────┴─────────┘
1,268 ┐ Male  8,535  11,407  Female
    ┌─────────────┬──────────────┐ 3,337
    │  27,500     │   29,495     │
    ├─────────────┼──────────────┤
    │             │              │
    │  25,824     │   20,755     │ Under 65
    └─────────────┴──────────────┘
     54,592         53,587
```

### Year 2015

```
1,903 ┐              7,918
    ┌──────────┬─────────┐
    │  9,668   │  7,126  │
    └──────────┴─────────┘
1,192 ┐ Male  11,986  15,325  Female
    ┌─────────────┬──────────────┐ 3,332
    │  24,576     │   27,118     │
    ├─────────────┼──────────────┤
    │             │              │
    │  26,004     │   19,799     │
    └─────────────┴──────────────┘
     51,772         50,249
```

**Notes:**

1. **Sources:** Both the 1960 and 1980 figures are based on the "Census" of the Statistics Bureau of the Prime Minister's Office, while the 2000 and 2015 figures are based on estimates by the Planning Bureau of the Economic Planning Agency.

span is longer than men's, the proportion of divorced or bereaved wives will increase particularly steeply as they get older.

As Figure 2-2-3 indicates, the composition of both espoused males and females will basically not change. However, because of an increase in average life span, the ratio of those espoused is expected to increase in old-aged generations. But a comparable ratio is expected to decline somewhat in middle-aged generations because of an increase in separations.

The absolute total number of separated or bereaved husbands and wives, aged 65 or over, will increase from 4,670,000 in 1980 to 7,250,000 in the year 2000 and 9,820,000 in 2015, because the population as a whole will become increasingly aged in the future. The number of divorced or bereaved wives will increase more sharply from 3,850,000 in 1980 to 6,010,000 in the year 2000 and 7,920,000 in 2015 (See Figure 2-2-4).

## Fig. 2-2-5 Changes in the Number of Students

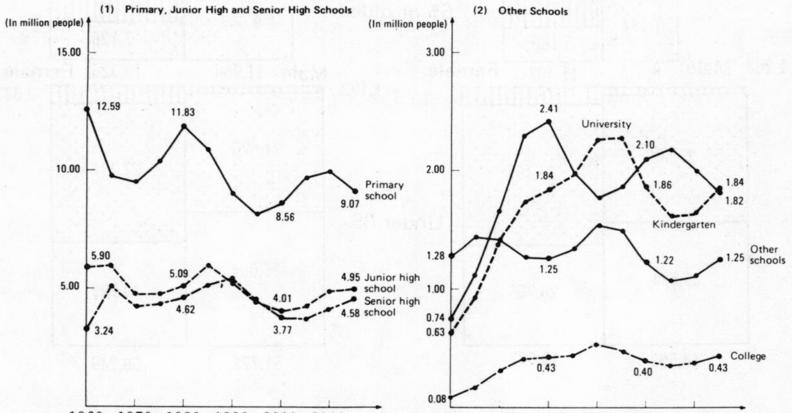

**Sources:** Education Ministry "Basic Survey on Schools" and estimates by the Planning Bureau of the Economic Planning Agency.

[Impact of Population Wave]

Future population changes in Japan will be influenced immensely by the postwar "baby boom" generation trends.

People born between 1947 and 1949 form a huge population mass that rises annually in the population pyramid. When these generations reached child-bearing age in 1971-73, they brought about the second "baby boom." A similar phenomenon will repeat itself every 25-30 years, though with waning impact. These population changes generate a population wave.

This population wave will bring about various economic and social impacts when it passes through each age bracket. One of these is the rapid aging of the population in the years leading up to the 21st century. A more easily predictable impact will be on school activity. As Figure 2-2-5 indicates, a peak number of children will move from primary school to junior high and senior high as the second "baby boom" generations pass by. A slightly lower third "baby boom" peak will appear in the 21st century.

This change in the number of school children will affect educational expenses and school facilities.

(2)  Households

Based on these assumptions, the following points may be noted about the future trends for households in Japan.

[Changes in Type of Household]

Household trends are apt to be determined by changes in the population and its age composition, changes in the husband-wife relationship according to sex and age, and changes in the pattern of household formation according to sex, age and spouse (to be referred to as the ratio of reversion to household).

Changes in the ratio of reversion to household in recent years clearly indicate (1) that the ratio of unmarried, separated or bereaved persons living with an unrelated family has been declining while the ratio of those forming one-person household has been increasing (an increase in the number of young or aged people who choose to live alone) and (2) that while there has been little change in the ratio of espoused females who live apart from their parents or married children, the ratio of those who live with relatives "other than their parents or children" has dropped significantly (purification of households).

Just how the ratio of reversion to household will change in future is hard to predict because it depends on a number of factors. Out prediction is based on the assumption that changes in the ratio in recent years will continue until the year 2000, and that these changes will diminish by half after that.

[Changes in the Number of Households and Household Patterns]

The increase in the number of ordinary households is expected to slacken, reflecting slower population growth. The total number will be 1.3 times the 1980 level in the year 2000 and 1.4 times that in 2015 (See Figure 2-2-6).

The following changes may take place in the pattern of household, as indicated in Figure 2-2-7.

In the first place, there will be a significant increase in the number of one-person households. The ratio of such households to the total number of households will rise from 15.8% in 1980 to 23.4% in the year 2000 and 27.8% in 2015. The absolute number of one-person households is also expected to increase drastically. Much of the increase will be due to the fact that more and more unmarried people or bereaved husbands and wives will choose to live alone. In particular, the number of aged women living alone will reach a level 2.5 times the present level in the year 2000 and 3.7 times that in 2015.

The ratio of nuclear families will remain high. The given share of households mainly composed of a couple and parents (or so-called three generation families) among relatives' households (ordinary households except for one-person households and non-relative households) will remain virtually unchanged at 20.9% in 1980s, 20.0% in the year 2000 and 21.0% in 2015. However, the share of nuclear family households — households composed of only a couple or a couple with children, households composed of a father with children and households composed of a mother with children — will increase slightly from 75.4% in 1980 to 78.2% in the year 2000 and 77.8% in 2015. The shares of both three-generation family households and nuclear family households in the total number of ordinary households will decline, because of an increase in the share of one-person households.

## Fig. 2-2-6 Changes in the Number of Ordinary Households

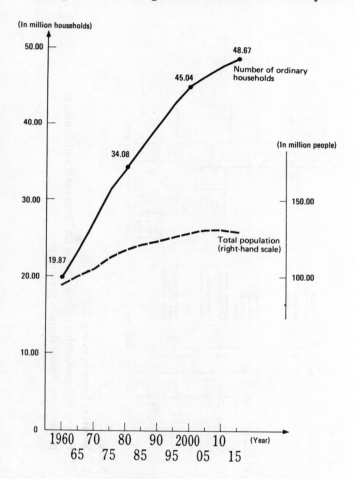

(In million households)

50.00

48.67

Number of ordinary households

45.04

40.00

34.08

(In million people)

30.00

150.00

Total population (right-hand scale)

19.87

20.00

100.00

10.00

0

1960 70 80 90 2000 10 (Year)
65 75 85 95 05 15

**Sources:** Statistics Bureau of the Prime Minister's Office "Census," Institute of Population Problems, the Health and Welfare Ministry "Future Population Projections for Japan by Sex-Age for 1980-2080" (November 1981) (medium variant used) and the estimates by the Planning Bureau of the Economic Planning Agency.

# Fig. 2-2-7　Changes in the Number of Households by Type

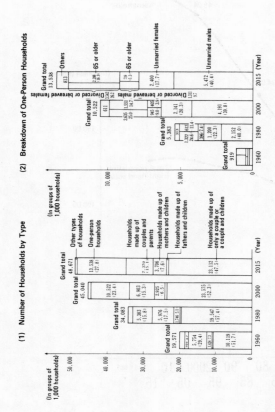

(1) Number of Households by Type

(2) Breakdown of One-Person Households

**Notes:**
1. **Sources:** Same as in Fig. 2-2-6.
2. Figures denote number of households (in thousands) and figures in parentheses denote share in percentage.

(3)    Regional Population Movements

Regional population movements were carried out on a large scale during he years of rapid economic growth. Amid the fast expanding economy and changing industrial structure, a large number of young people in the country left their families and moved to big cities. In recent years, however, as people choose to settle down, population movements have gradually slowed down, and the population concentration in cities has almost come to an end (See Figure 2-2-8). The following points may be noted about future population movements.

[Greater Trend Toward Settling Down]
One main point in recent years is a gradual decline in movements and a growing trend among people to settle down. The number of lifetime removals (the frequency of a person moving from one place to another in his lifetime) dropped to 6.6 in 1980 from 7.7 in 1970. This growing trend to settle in one place is expected to continue for the following reasons.
First, the ratio of eldest sons or daughters to the total number of children will continue to increase. As an indicator of this trend, we use the ratio of the youth population to parent population, which is the alternate generation index (obtained from the population of people aged between 15 and 24 divided by the population of those aged between 40 and 49). As shown in Figure 2-2-9, the index dropped from 1.8 in 1965 to 1.0 in 1970. The index is likely to remain below 1 over the years leading up to the 21st century. This means that the number of young people is almost equal to the number of their parents, which is close to the marginal level needed to ensure an alternate generation in a household. This state will continue in future.
Second, there are fewer economic factors that will prompt population movements. As the income gaps on a regional basis narrow, fewer people will necessarily have to move from one region to another for economic or occupational reasons. This trend will continue over the coming years.

[Coexistence of Settling Down and High Mobility]
Despite the general trend towards settling down, there will still be

## Fig. 2-2-8 Changes in the Pattern of Population Movements

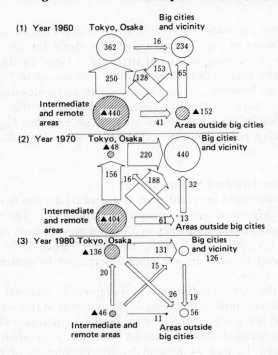

**Notes:**

1. **Source:** Statistics Bureau of the Prime Minister's Office "Report on Movements of Population Registered in the Ledger."
2. Figures denote actual number of persons (in thousands).
3. Definition of areas is as follows:

| Area | Prefectures covered |
|---|---|
| Tokyo. Osaka | Tokyo. Osaka |
| Big cities and vicinity | Saitama. Chiba. Kanagawa. Aichi. Mie. Kyoto. Hyogo |
| Areas outside big cities | Ibaraki. Tochigi. Gunma. Shizuoka. Shiga. Nara. Wakayama. Okayama. Hiroshima. Yamaguchi. Fukuoka. Oita |
| Intermediate areas | Miyagi. Yamagata. Fukushima. Niigata. Toyama. Ishikawa. Fukui. Yamanashi. Nagano. Gifu. Tottori. Shimane. Tokushima. Kagawa. Ehime. Kochi |
| Remote areas | Hokkaido. Aomori. Iwate. Akita. Saga. Nagasaki. Kumamoto. Miyagi. Kagoshima. Okinawa |

## Fig. 2-2-9 Population Concentration in Cities, Income Gaps, and Population of the Young

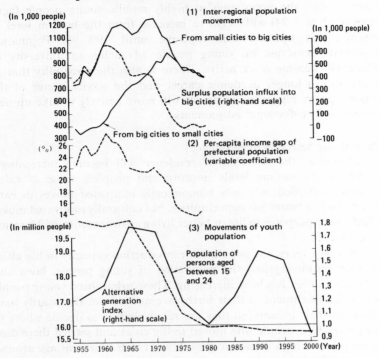

**Notes:**

1. **Sources:** Figures are based on the "Report on Movements of Population Registered on the Ledger" and "Census" of the Statistics Bureau of the Prime Minister's Office, "Prefectural Income Statistics" of the Economic Planning Agency, and the medium variant in "Future Population Projections for Japan by Sex-Age for 1980-2080" (November 1981) of the Institute of Population Problems, the Ministry of Health and Welfare.

2. Big city areas here mean Saitama, Chiba, Tokyo, Kanagawa, Aichi, Mie, Kyoto, Osaka and Hyogo prefectures.

3. The alternate generation index is the figure given when the population of those aged between 15 and 24 is divided by the population of those aged between 40 and 49.

the possibility of a certain segment of people actively choosing to move from one place to another. As the second "baby boom" generations become older, the population of highly mobile young people (aged between 15 and 24) will begin to increase from the bottom level at present. This uptrend will continue until 1990-95. Population movements centering on young people advancing to university or college will become more active. There is also the possibility that as people seek a longer academic career and the service sector of the economy grows bigger, more people will move actively to take up new business and professional assignments.

[Diversifying Selection of Residence]

In future, the selection of residence will become increasingly diversified. As income levels improve and people's sense of value becomes diversified, not only economically motivated moves to earn more money or better job opportunities, but culturally motivated moves to find better purposes in life or better living environments, will become more frequent.

In recent years, the population reproduction capacity in big cities has been improving and the population of young people, born and grown up in cities, has been increasing. These urban-bred young people have little attachment to their birthplace and do not necessarily have to succeed their parents, so they are relatively free to decide where to live. Meanwhile, people who moved to big cities and settled there during the years of high economic growth will reach retirment age around the year 2000. Where these people will decide to live after their retirement may greatly affect future population movements.

[Future Population Distribution]

It is hard to predict at the present moment how population distribution will change as a result of such a diversified selection of residence by people. This study will give two estimates of Japan's geographical population distribution in the year 2000 — one based on the assumption that there will be no social increase or decrease in population (closed-type population estimate), and another based on the assumption that there will be an increase or decrease similar to the one seen between 1975 and 1980 (mobile-type population estimate) (See Table 2-2-10).

## Table 2-2-10　Area-wise Estimate of Future Population

(In 10,000 people, %)

| | Year 1980 | | Year 2000 | | | |
| | | | Closed-type estimate | | Mobile-type estimate | |
| | Population | Share | Population | Share | Population | Share |
|---|---|---|---|---|---|---|
| Hokkaido | 556 | 4.8 | 609 | 4.8 | 581 | 4.5 |
| Northern Tohoku | 420 | 3.6 | 459 | 3.6 | 419 | 3.3 |
| Southern Tohoku | 779 | 6.7 | 846 | 6.6 | 794 | 6.2 |
| Inland Kanto | 908 | 7.8 | 988 | 7.7 | 1,009 | 7.9 |
| Coastal Kanto | 2,864 | 24.5 | 3,182 | 24.8 | 3,465 | 27.0 |
| Tokai | 1,334 | 11.4 | 1,487 | 11.6 | 1,464 | 11.4 |
| Hokuriku | 299 | 2.6 | 320 | 2.5 | 295 | 2.3 |
| Inland Kinki | 480 | 4.1 | 519 | 4.1 | 572 | 4.5 |
| Coastal Kinki | 1,475 | 12.6 | 1,624 | 12.7 | 1,526 | 11.9 |
| Sanin | 140 | 1.2 | 144 | 1.1 | 139 | 1.1 |
| Sanyo | 619 | 5.3 | 657 | 5.1 | 618 | 4.8 |
| Shikoku | 416 | 3.6 | 435 | 3.4 | 415 | 3.2 |
| Northern Kyushu | 824 | 7.0 | 897 | 7.0 | 878 | 6.9 |
| Southern Kyushu | 580 | 5.0 | 645 | 5.0 | 637 | 5.0 |
| All areas | 11,692 | 100.0 | 12,812 | 100.0 | 12,812 | 100.0 |
| (Three big city areas) | (5,673) | (48.5) | (6,293) | (49.1) | (6,455) | (50.4) |

**Notes:**
1. Figures are based on the "Census" of the Statistics Bureau of the Prime Minister's Office and the estimates of the Planning Bureau of the Economic Planning Agency.
2. Figures for "All areas" conform to the medium variant in "Future Population Projections for Japan by Sex-Age for 1980-2080" (November 1981) of the Institute of Population Problems, the Ministry of Health and Welfare.
3. "Closed-type" estimates are based on the assumption that there will be no social change in the population. "Mobile-type" estimates are based on the assumption that the rate of movements in the 1975-80 period will remain unchanged.
4. Area definition is as follows:
   Hokkaido = Hokkaido
   Northern Tohoku = Aomori, Iwate, Akita
   Southern Tohoku = Miyagi, Yamagata, Fukushima, Niigata
   Inland Kanto = Ibaraki, Tochigi, Gunma, Yamanashi, Nagano
   Coastal Kanto = Saitama, Chiba, Tokyo, Kanagawa
   Tokai = Shizuoka, Aichi, Gifu, Mie
   Hokuriku = Toyama, Ishikawa, Fukui
   Inland Kinki = Shiga, Kyoto, Nara
   Coastal Kinki = Osaka, Hyogo, Wakayama
   Sanin = Tottori, Shimane
   Sanyo = Okayama, Hiroshima, Yamaguchi
   Shikoku = Tokushima, Kagawa, Ehime, Kochi
   Northern Kyushu = Fukuoka, Saga, Nagasaki, Oita
   Southern Kyushu = Kumamoto, Miyazaki, Kagoshima, Okinawa
   Three big city areas = Coastal Kanto, Tokai, Coastal Kinki

According to the closed-type estimate, urban regions will have a slightly bigger share in the year 2000 of population distribution than at present. This is because while the birth rate will be lower in urban regions than rural regions, the natural increase in population will be slightly higher in the former since the share of the population of child-bearing women will be relatively larger there. However, the actual growth of population in the big cities will slow down significantly, and the proportion of elderly people to total urban population will fast increase in the 1990s.

According to the mobile-type estimate, the population will tend to concentrate in big cities. The younger generations, born during the second "baby boom" years, will move in large numbers to the cities, and some rural regions may experience a drop in population.

## 2. Economy

### (1) Economic Growth

[Fundamental View of Economic Growth]
During the two-decade period leading up to the 21st century, Japan will be able to maintain somewhat higher economic growth than other industrially advanced countries, if it can succeed in retaining its economic vitality in such a manner as suggested in Chapter 3. This is because Japan will continue to enjoy better growth conditions than other countries. For one thing, Japan's ratio of productive population will remain high by international standards. For another, as we will see later in this section, the drop in the savings ratio will be much slower in Japan.

As indicated by the results of a poll (hereafter referred to as the Delphi poll) which the Economic Planning Agency conducted for this study (See Figure 2-2-11), the biggest percentage of those who responded estimated Japan's average annual growth rate between 1981 and the year 2000 at higher than 4%. In fact, about 90% of the respondents mentioned growth rates between 3% and just over 5%.

Growth incentives mentioned most frequently by them included "progress in technology," "private investment in equipment" and "the quality of labor and worker morale." "International industrial adjustment and trade friction," "oil supply trends" and "trends for the

## Fig. 2-2-11    Future Economic Growth Rates

### (1)  Presumed Real Annual Growth Rate (1981 — 2000)

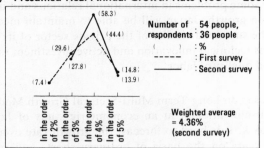

Number of respondents : 54 people, 36 people
(       )   : %
- - - -   : First survey
———   : Second survey

Weighted average = 4.36% (second survey)

### (2)  Growth Factors Mentioned

| Item | Positive factors | Negative factors |
|---|---|---|
| Oil supply trends | (1.9)<br>(2.8) | (57.4)<br>(72.2) |
| Trends for supply of non-oil resources and energy | (9.3)<br>(11.1) | (18.5)<br>(30.6) |
| Trend for industrial siting | (1.9)<br>(2.8) | (9.3)<br>(5.6) |
| Population and labor trends | (9.3)<br>(5.6) | (33.3)<br>(30.6) |
| Trend for work hours | (0.0)<br>(0.0) | (18.5)<br>(16.7) |
| Quality of labor and workers' morale | (38.9)<br>(50.0) | (20.4)<br>(19.4) |
| Trend for personal savings | (20.4)<br>(16.7) | (1.9)<br>(5.6) |
| Trend for private investment in plants and equipment | (63.0)<br>(80.6) | (0.0)<br>(0.0) |
| Trend for investment in anti-pollution facilities | (3.7)<br>(5.6) | (0.0)<br>(0.0) |
| Inflation trend | (9.3)<br>(0.3) | (22.2)<br>(30.6) |
| Trend for personal consumption expenditure | (22.2)<br>(13.9) | (3.7)<br>(0.0) |
| Trend for technological progress | (81.5)<br>(97.2) | (7.4)<br>(0.0) |
| Trend for government spending on social welfare | (1.9)<br>(2.8) | (7.4)<br>(8.3) |
| Trend for official actions, like control and intervention | (7.4)<br>(5.6) | (7.4)<br>(0.0) |
| Trends for international industrial adjustment and trade friction | (0.0)<br>(0.0) | (63.0)<br>(75.0) |
| Other factors | (0.0)<br>(0.0) | (1.9)<br>(5.6) |

Number of respondents : 54 people, 36 people
(       )   : %
Top figures   : First survey
Bottom figures   : Second survey

**Source:**  Economic Planning Agency "Survey on National Life 20 Years Hence."

population and labor force" were most frequently cited as deterrents to growth. In other words, the typical replies in the poll seem to suggest that despite some problems in international relations and in the pattern of population growth, Japan will be able to maintain medium growth thanks to the sustained vitality of the private sector of its economy, in such areas as technical innovation and active investment in equipment, and the good quality of labor.

[Outlook Based on Long-Term Multi-Sectoral Growth Model]

We will now attempt at an econometric study of Japan's future growth outlook. It is hard to forecast the growth rate over a period as long as 20 years on the basis of ordinary short- and medium-term econometric models. Our outlook, therefore, will be based on a long-term multi-sectoral growth model (also known as the turnpike model).

This model is designed to probe future economic potential. It is primarily aimed at studying how capital, labor and other resources should be distributed in order to obtain the maximum quantity of final consumption and services from social overhead capital over the next 20 years. The industrial structure as envisaged by this model provides a formula under which resources can be distributed efficiently at different times, capital equipment fully operated and goods and services utilized to the full.

Therefore, the model provides a course of maximum possible growth and provides a clue for judging how efficient the present state of the economy is.

In setting up this model, trends for the population and labor force, trends for technical progress in each industry, terms of trade, dependence on imports and trade friction, and formation of necessary stock in the 21st century were considered as factors that can restrict economic growth. It should be noted that there can be various assumptions concerning each of these factors.

A course of economic growth thus obtained is given as Case F. In reality, however, it is hard to see that capital equipment is fully operated and various resources utilized 100% efficiently. Therefore, a growth course, provided that the operation of capital equipment remains at the average level of the past (between 1968 and 1979 excluding the two years, 1974 and 1975, immediately after the first oil crisis), is given in Case I.

[Growth Rate Suggested by the Model]

According to our calculations, the real economic growth rate between 1980 and the year 2000 will average around 4.4% a year in Case F and around 4.0% in Case I.

Because of considerable changes in the relative prices of goods, the real growth rate over a long period of time can be much different, depending on which year is taken as the base year. To eliminate such factors, the growth rates given above have been computed by shifting the base years in turn (which may be called chain growth rates).

An item-wise breakdown of the growth rate from the demand side, as shown in Table 2-2-12, suggests that (1) the growth rate of final consumption expenditure will be relatively high, (2) while fixed capital formation will steadily increase, its weight will somewhat decline partly because of slower economic growth and partly because of a gradual drop in the overall capital coefficient due to changes in the industrial structure, and (3) although housing investment will steadily increase to ensure a qualitative improvement in houses, its weight will also diminish because of a slower population growth rate.

Taking into consideration other factors that will support economic growth, such as the savings rate, technical innovations and supply of labor, and assuming the future of the world economy as discussed in Section 1 of this chapter, we envisage an annual growth rate of around 4% over the next 20 years. The world economy is now in a very difficult phase and there are many uncertain factors that may affect Japan's future economic growth. It should be remembered that Japan's future growth rate may prove much different depending on world economic developments over the coming years. The growth rate suggested above, therefore, should be viewed with considerable latitude.

(2)  Savings and Investment

[Reasons for High Savings Rate]

The savings rate (particularly the household savings rate) in Japan has been considerably higher than in other countries. This, combined with vigorous corporate investment, has prompted the rapid development of the Japanese economy. How the savings rate changes in future will greatly affect Japan's economic development.

There are several factors behind Japan's high savings rate. First,

## Table 2-2-12　The Outlook for the Demand Structure

| | Actual value at 1975 prices (in trillion yen, %) | | | | Average annual growth rate (%) | | Nominal value (in trillion yen, %) | | | |
|---|---|---|---|---|---|---|---|---|---|---|
| | 1960 | 1970 | 1980 | 2000 | 1960~ 1980 | 1980~ 2000 | 1960 | 1970 | 1980 | 2000 |
| Final consumption expenditure | 33.4 (76.9) | 75.9 (64.4) | 119.0 (63.0) | 279.2 (64.9) | 6.6 | 4.4 | 10.6 (65.9) | 43.7 (59.7) | 160.3 (68.2) | (70.5) |
| Capital formation | 10.8 (24.9) | 44.6 (37.8) | 62.3 (33.0) | 130.8 (30.4) | 9.2 | 3.8 | 5.4 (33.4) | 28.6 (39.0) | 76.8 (32.7) | (29.0) |
| Net exports of goods and services | -0.8 (-1.8) | -2.7 (-2.3) | 7.5 (4.0) | 20.0 (4.7) | — | — | 0.1 (0.6) | 0.9 (1.3) | -2.1 (-0.9) | (0.5) |
| Gross domestic expenditure | 43.5 | 117.8 | 188.8 | 430.0 | 7.6 | 4.2 | 16.1 | 73.3 | 234.9 | (100.0) |
| Chain growth rate | | | | | | 4.0 | | | | |

**Notes:**

1. Figures are based on "Annual Report on National Accounts (New SNA)" of the Economic Planning Agency and the estimates of the Planning Bureau of the Economic Planning Agency.

2. This table gives demand estimates under the long-term multi-sectoral growth model. Unlike conventional demand estimates, they are not based on income factors.

3. Breakdown of items:

   Final consumption expenditure = private final consumption expenditure + government final consumption expenditure

   Capital formation = gross domestic capital formation

   Net exports of goods and services = surplus of the national current account − factor income received from abroad + factor income paid abroad

4. Figures in parentheses denote shares.

personal income has increased at a pace much faster than people generally anticipated. Second, people have been very enthusiastic about increasing their financial assets and owning house. Third, younger generations have been eager to save money to provide for their old age and for their children's education. Fourth, poor social welfare has induced people to save money for emergencies and life after retirement. Fifth, saving has been traditionally considered a virtue, and this has been enhanced by unique summer and winter bonus payments.

[Household Savings Rate to Decline Moderately]

In future, however, the household savings rate is expected to decline moderately for the following reasons.

In the first place, the growth of household disposable income will gradually slow down. Rapid increases in disposable income as in the past will be hard to come by any more, as the people will have to bear greater burdens amid slower economic growth.

The second reason is the growing share of aged people in the total population. Individual households usually adjust income and expenditure, taking their life cycle into consideration. Normally they tend to save money while their family members are engaged in productive activity and live on their savings after retirement. If the pattern of saving in individual households remains unchanged, a bigger share of aged people in the population composition will mean a lower savings rate.

Third, there will be a maturing of social welfare, particularly public pensions. More households will take pensions for granted and find less need to save for their old age. This leads to a lower savings rate.

Fourth, there will be further improvement in individual financial assets and housing stock. This reduces the motive to save.

On the other hand, however, the proportion of aged workers will remain high and the people will generally remain eager to seek a qualitative improvement in their houses. In the transit period leading up to an aged society, people may choose to save more to provide for life after retirement. There will also be an increase in the number of people who get retirement allowances. These factors may act to raise the savings rate.

Therefore, the household savings rate is not likely to decline

**Fig. 2-2-13   Household Savings Rate: Past Trends and Future Outlook**

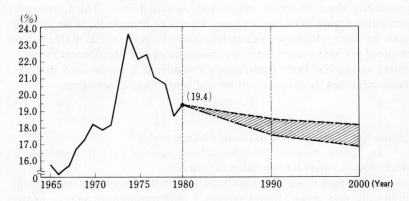

**Notes:**
1. **Sources:** Economic Planning Agency "Annual Report on National Accounts" and estimates of the Planning Bureau of the Economic Planning Agency.
2. All figures are on a new SNA basis.

greatly until around the year 2000, and the savings rate is expected to remain higher in Japan than in other advanced countries.

[How Much the Savings Rate Will Decline]

An estimate of how much the savings rate will decline over the coming years is illustrated in Figure 2-2-13. The levels of disposable income, financial stock and pensions have been taken into account in giving this estimate. The figure shows that Japan's household savings rate, as computed on a new SNA (system of national accounts) basis, will decline by some 2 percentage points from 19.4% in 1980 to 16-17% in the year 2000.

The ratio of the net balance of household financial assets to total disposable income will rise from 1.2 in 1980 to around 1.5 in the year 2000.

In the⁻ Delphi survey (See Figure 2-2-14), most respondents predicted that the household savings rate (based on a household

### Fig. 2-2-14 Savings Rate: Past Trends and Future Outlook

#### (1) Past Savings Rate Trend

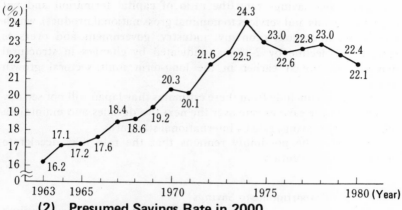

#### (2) Presumed Savings Rate in 2000

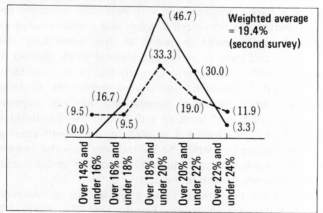

Weighted average
= 19.4%
(second survey)

Number of respondents : 42 people, 30 people

( ) : %

----- : First survey

——— : Second survey

**Sources:** Statistics Bureau of the Prime Minister's Office "Family Income and Expenditure Survey" and Economic Planning Agency "Survey on National Life 20 Years Hence."

economy survey covering workers' households throughout Japan) will fall from 22.1% in 1980 to a level "somewhere between 18% and 20%" (19.4% on the weighted average) in the year 2000.

The gross savings rate (the ratio of capital formation and net exports of goods and services to nominal gross national product), which covers the household economy, industry, government and overseas sector, will decline by 2-3%, as indicated by changes in structural demand mentioned earlier in the long-term multi-sectoral growth model.

One may conclude from these estimates that Japan will not see any major fall in the savings rate over the next two decades and maintain a relatively high savings rate by international standards.

However, the possibility remains that the rate may decelerate faster in the 21st century.


[Investment Proportionate to Savings]

Corporate investment in new plants and equipment may continue to increase at a pace commensurate with moderate economic growth, provided the industry is convinced of long- and medium-range growth prospects and improvement is made in the investment climate. However, the overall capital coefficient (capital stock divided by the value of output) will either remain virtually flat or decline. Increased energy-saving and labor-saving investment may work to raise the coefficient, but future technical innovations that can improve the productivity of capital will work to pull it downwards. Besides, the capital coefficient is relatively low in such future growth areas as the electronics and service industries. So the industry's overinvestment will not be able to absorb surplus household savings as it did during the years of high economic growth in the past.

Enthusiasm for investment to seek qualitative improvement of houses is expected to remain strong. Over the next 20 to 30 years, Japan needs to improve and build up social overhead capital so that a safer and more comfortable living environment can be passed on to future generations.

Japan's relatively high savings rate means that it can set aside more money for investment. The next two decades will be a period in which Japan can accumulate good quality national stock by trying to create investment opportunities that will absorb the growth in savings.

(3)    Development of Technology

[Development of Technology as Propellant of Economic and Social Progress]
　　Since history began, technical innovation has been a major propellant of economic and social development and the key to the door of the future. Technical innovation has accelerated in various fields since the turn of the century and has made a great contribution to the formation of today's rich materialistic culture.
　　Some examples of technical achievements include chemical fertilizer developed from fixing nitrogen in the air, high polymer chemicals like nylon, automobiles, aircraft, transistors, integrated circuits and computers. The way has also been opened for the peaceful use of nuclear energy and space.
　　In future, technical innovation will continue to play a major role in the progress of economic society.

[Japan's Technical Development at High Level]
　　In postwar years, Japan has not only positively introduced technologies from industrially advanced Western countries and improved them, but also endeavored to develop its own technology. As a result, the technology of Japanese industry has attained one of the highest levels in almost all areas with the exception of a segment of high technology fields.
　　Japanese products, supported by these high-level technologies, have won a high reputation worldwide for their reliable quality, good after-sales service and punctual delivery.
　　The industries' incessant efforts to improve existing technologies, the importance the Japanese attach to "harmony" which has brought about close partnerships between those engaged in technological development and production for the quality improvement of products, and fierce competition between businesses may be cited as factors behind the rapid technical development in Japan.

[Outlook for Japan's Technology Development]
　　There are various stages in technological development. A technical classification provides five different stages: (1) improved technology, (2) applied technology, (3) high technology, (4) future technology, and (5)

innovative technology. It may be said that Japan reached international standards in improved technology in the late 1950s, in applied technology in the late 1960s, and in much of the high technology in the latter part of the 1970s. However, the general assessment is that it has not yet attained international standards in both the future technology and innovative technology categories.

Over the coming years, Japan, making good use of its attributes, will actively continue technical development centering on mechatronic technology. By concentrating its energy on the development of creative technology, Japan will be able to make a great contribution to the future development of not only its own economy but the world economy as well.

[New Frontier of Technology]

The frontier of technical development will expand over the coming years to involve a wide range of fields.

Here is an outlook on Japan's involvement in high-technology fields.

In the field of energy, solar cells, fuel cells and new-type batteries will be put into practical use in the 1990s. The development of technology related to nuclear fusion may not come until after the year 2000. Technological development in the electronics field will progress rapidly, bringing an optical-fiber communications system, high-performance integrated circuits and many other sophisticated products to practical use. Among other practical achievements before the year 2000 will be drugs based on gene restructuring technology, artificial organs, space laboratories, low-noise, short takeoff and landing aircraft, the recovery of uranium from sea water, the recovery of manganese nodules from sea beds, new transport systems, linear motor trains and a sophisticated information network system.

(4)  Energy

Japan's economic performance has been jolted by the two global oil crises. The future of the Japanese economy will continue to depend much on how the world energy situation changes and how Japan can cope with such changes.

We will now study the prospects for Japan's energy supply and demand on the assumption that Japan will attain an annual economic growth rate of around 4%.

[Energy-Saving Efforts and Energy Demand]

Japan has made remarkable progress in energy conservation since the first oil crisis. As a result, Japan's energy consumption per unit of GNP has declined significantly. Industry has accounted for much of the energy-saving efforts. Energy-saving that began in various industrial sectors after the first oil crisis entered a second phase after the second oil crisis. Large-scale investment in energy-saving facilities is now in progress.

However, energy-saving investment so far has been prompted primarily by the increase in oil prices and concentrated on facilities based on the application of existing technology.

Energy-saving will make further progress in Japan, encouraged by

**Fig. 2-2-15   The Outlook for Primary Energy Consumption per Unit of GNP**

(Year 1980 = 100)

**Sources:**   Agency of Natural Resources and Energy, MITI "Comprehensive Energy Statistics" and estimates of the Planning Bureau of the Economic Planning Agency.

various government policies. However, with energy consumption in the private sector likely to increase, and with no remarkable expansion of energy-saving facilities based on existing technology expected in the coming years, energy-saving in terms of energy consumption per unit of GNP will gradually slow down as shown in Figure 2-2-15.

As a result, assuming that the Japanese economy will grow at an annual rate of around 4%, total energy demand will increase from the crude oil equivalent of 429 million kiloliters in 1980 to 690 million kiloliters in the year 2000.

[Energy Supply and Balance Between Demand and Supply]
We see the prospects for the energy supply as follows:
(1) The volume of oil Japan can secure will not increase much beyond the present level of 5 million barrels per day (290 million kiloliters). This is because while there will be no substantial increase in the world's total oil supply, an increase in oil demand in developing countries is seen to be unavoidable.
(2) There will be an increase in steaming coal imports, mainly by electric power companies, as coal will retain its competitive edge over oil.
(3) Nuclear power generation as an alternative energy source should be introduced to the extent a balanced supply of power permits. However, much effort will be needed to realize this in view of siting difficulties and the long time required for the construction of a nuclear power plant.
(4) There will be a steady increase in the volume of liquefied natural gas (LNG) consumed. But the volume of LNG consumed by electric power companies, which increased in the 1980s, will tend to level off in the 1990s.
(5) As to other new energy sources, there will be continued progress in the development of coal liquefaction, fuel alcohol and solar energy.

These assumptions lead to the estimate of Japan's energy demand and supply as given in Table 2-2-16.

# Table 2-2-16　The Outlook for the Primary Energy Supply-Demand Balance

| Fiscal year | 1980 | | 2000 | | | | | |
| --- | --- | --- | --- | --- | --- | --- | --- | --- |
| | Actual demand | | Case 1 | | Case 2 | | Case 3 | |
| Average annual economic growth rate (1980-2000) (%) | — | | 3.0 | | 4.0 | | 4.5 | |
| Total primary energy demand (in 100 million kl) | 4.29 | | 5.72 | | 6.94 | | 7.64 | |
| Type of energy | Actual supplies | Shares | Actual supplies | Shares | Actual supplies | Shares | Actual supplies | Shares |
| Hydroelectric power (general) (in 10,000 kW) | 1,900 | } 5.6 | 3,000 | } 6.5 | 3,000 | } 5.4 | 3,000 | } 4.9 |
| Hydroelectric power (pumping) (in 10,000 kW) | 1,080 | | 3,350 | | 3,350 | | 3,350 | |
| Geothermal (in 10,000 kW) | 16 (300,000 kl) | 0.1 | 700 | 2.5 | 700 | 2.1 | 700 | 1.8 |
| Domestic oil and natural gas (in 10,000 kl) | 270 | 0.6 | 1,400 | 2.4 | 1,400 | 2.0 | 1,400 | 1.8 |
| Nuclear power (in 10,000 kW) | 1,570 | 5.0 | 6,000 ~8,000 | 15.8 ~21.0 | 7,500 ~9,500 | 16.2 ~20.6 | 8,000 ~10,000 | 15.8 ~19.7 |
| LNG (in 10,000 tons) | 1,680 | 5.5 | 4,800 | 12.0 | 4,800 | 9.9 | 4,800 | 9.0 |
| Coal (in 10,000 tons) | 9,240 | 16.7 | 15,200 | 19.7 | 17,200 | 18.2 | 18,400 | 17.7 |
| New energy, etc. (in 10,000 kl) | 70 | 0.2 | 3,500 ~6,000 | 6.1 ~10.5 | 4,500 ~7,500 | 6.5 ~10.8 | 5,500 ~8,000 | 7.2 ~10.5 |
| Total (in 100 million kl) | 1.44 | 33.7 | 3.72 ~4.27 | 65.0 ~74.6 | 4.18 ~4.79 | 60.3 ~69.0 | 4.45 ~5.00 | 58.2 ~65.4 |
| Imported oil (including LPG) (in 100 million kl) | 2.85 | 66.3 | 2.00 ~1.45 | 35.0 ~25.4 | 2.76 ~2.15 | 39.7 ~31.0 | 3.19 ~2.64 | 41.8 ~34.6 |

**Notes:**
1. Based on the estimates of the Planning Bureau of the Economic Planning Agency.
2. This table is simply designed to give a broad picture of Japan's energy supply and demand in the year 2000.

(5)  Industrial Structure

[Increasing Importance of Software]
Against the background of medium economic growth, industrial society in Japan will inevitably undergo rapid changes brought about by the surging wave of internationalization, the people's diversifying needs, and technological progress.

Different expressions such as "knowledge intensification," "cultural industrialization," "systematization," and "servicization" have been invented to characterize future industrial society. None of them seem to be good enough to describe exactly what is actually going on at present in Japanese industrial society.

We suggest an expression "softwarization" to describe a general trend, in which "software" such as knowledge and services is given a relatively higher appraisal than "hardware" such as goods and resources.

This "softwarization" may progress in various forms. For example, it may present itself in the form of an increased number of knowledge-intensive and service businesses. It will grow strong in the area of "goods" (like fashion), and in the same industry, sales of software (like software in the computer industry) will grow faster than sales of hardware.

As consumption becomes more personal and diversified, and as the labor force is increasingly assigned to more sophisticated and creative work, and with the supply of energy and resources expected to remain restrictive, the trend towards "softwarization" will be inevitable and desirable for Japan.


[Image of Future Industrial Structure]
We will try to visualize what Japan's future industrial structure will look like, based on the long-term multi-sectoral growth model (Case I) mentioned earlier in this chapter (See Table 2-2-17).

Over a period as long as 20 years, the image of the industrial structure will differ much, according to whether it is viewed in real terms (on the basis of products) or in nominal terms (on the basis of added value incorporating changes in relative prices).

In real terms, there will be spectacular growth in the machinery and service industries. The machinery industry will enjoy strong

## Table 2-2-17 The Outlook for the Industrial Structure

**(1) Real**

| Industry | Real gross domestic product at 1975 price (in trillion yen, %) | | | Average annual increase rate (%) | |
|---|---|---|---|---|---|
| | 1970 | 1980 | 2000 | 1970~1980 | 1980~2000 |
| Primary industry | 7.1 | 7.1 | 9.2 | 0.0 | 1.3 |
| | ( 6.1) | ( 3.7) | ( 2.1) | | |
| Secondary industry | 46.3 | 82.1 | 198.2 | 5.9 | 4.5 |
| | ( 39.7) | ( 42.3) | ( 46.1) | | |
| Mining and manufacturing | 35.7 | 67.4 | 170.9 | 6.6 | 4.8 |
| | ( 30.5) | ( 34.7) | ( 39.7) | | |
| Chemicals | 7.5 | 10.7 | 15.0 | 3.6 | 1.7 |
| | ( 6.4) | ( 5.5) | ( 3.5) | | |
| Primary metals | 3.4 | 7.2 | 9.2 | 7.8 | 1.2 |
| | ( 3.0) | ( 3.7) | ( 2.1) | | |
| Machinery | 13.2 | 33.7 | 124.1 | 9.8 | 6.1 |
| | ( 11.3) | ( 17.4) | ( 28.9) | | |
| Others | 11.6 | 15.8 | 22.6 | 3.1 | 1.8 |
| | ( 9.9) | ( 8.1) | ( 5.2) | | |
| Construction | 10.7 | 14.7 | 27.3 | 3.2 | 3.2 |
| | ( 9.1) | ( 7.6) | ( 6.4) | | |
| Tertiary industry | 63.4 | 104.8 | 222.5 | 5.2 | 3.8 |
| | ( 54.3) | ( 54.0) | ( 51.8) | | |
| Electricity, gas, water | 2.6 | 3.8 | 5.7 | 3.9 | 2.0 |
| | ( 2.2) | ( 2.0) | ( 1.3) | | |
| Finance, insurance, real estate | 13.6 | 27.7 | 55.0 | 7.4 | 3.8 |
| | ( 11.6) | ( 14.3) | ( 13.5) | | |
| Transportation, communication | 7.1 | 11.3 | 18.0 | 4.8 | 2.3 |
| | ( 6.1) | ( 5.8) | ( 4.2) | | |
| Services, etc. | 40.1 | 62.0 | 140.9 | 4.5 | 4.2 |
| | ( 34.4) | ( 31.9) | ( 32.8) | | |
| Total | 116.8 | 194.1 | 430.0 | 5.2 | 4.1 |
| | (100.0) | (100.0) | (100.0) | | |
| Statistical errors | 1.0 | −5.3 | — | | |
| Gross domestic product | 117.8 | 188.8 | 430.0 | 4.8 | 4.2 |
| Chain growth rate | | | | 5.0 | 4.0 |

**Table 2-2-17 cont'd**

(2) **Nominal**

| Industry | Nominal gross domestic product (in trillion yen, %) | | |
|---|---|---|---|
| | 1970 | 1980 | 2000 |
| Primary industry | 4.4 | 8.6 | |
| | ( 6.0) | ( 3.7) | ( 4.2) |
| Secondary industry | 31.6 | 89.6 | |
| | ( 43.1) | ( 38.2) | ( 31.5) |
| Mining and manufacturing | 26.2 | 68.8 | |
| | ( 35.7) | ( 29.3) | ( 21.6) |
| Chemicals | 5.8 | 12.7 | |
| | ( 7.9) | ( 5.4) | ( 1.5) |
| Primary metals | 2.9 | 8.4 | |
| | ( 3.9) | ( 3.6) | ( 0.8) |
| Machinery | 10.1 | 28.0 | |
| | ( 13.7) | ( 11.9) | ( 15.7) |
| Others | 7.4 | 19.6 | |
| | ( 10.1) | ( 8.4) | ( 3.6) |
| Construction | 5.5 | 20.9 | |
| | ( 7.4) | ( 8.9) | ( 10.0) |
| Tertiary industry | 37.3 | 136.5 | |
| | ( 50.9) | ( 58.1) | ( 64.2) |
| Electricity, gas, water | 1.6 | 7.1 | |
| | ( 2.2) | ( 3.0) | ( 1.5) |
| Finance, insurance, real estate | 9.3 | 36.5 | |
| | ( 12.6) | ( 15.5) | ( 8.5) |
| Transportation, communication | 4.9 | 15.5 | |
| | ( 6.6) | ( 6.6) | ( 5.6) |
| Services, etc. | 21.6 | 77.4 | |
| | ( 29.4) | ( 33.0) | ( 48.6) |
| Total | 73.4 | 234.8 | |
| | (100.0) | (100.0) | (100.0) |
| Statistical errors | −0.1 | 0.2 | |
| Gross domestic product | 73.3 | 234.9 | |

**Notes:**
1. Based on "Annual Report on National Accounts (New SNA)" of the Economic Planning Agency and the estimates by the Planning Bureau of the Economic Planning Agency.
2. Nominal figures for the year 2000 are based on the shadow prices of goods drawn from the long-term multi-sectoral growth model.
3. Figures in parentheses denote shares in percentage.

demand related to the investment in labor-saving and energy-saving facilities and sustained export demand. In the service industry, a major increase can be expected both in intermediate and final demand.

In the manufacturing sector, production output of the primary metal industry will not grow much because of a general shift to smaller and lighter machinery and a decline in export demand. Production growth in "other manufacturing industries" will be modest in the face of increasing imports from developing countries. Therefore, the priority in the manufacturing sector will clearly shift from the basic materials industries like chemicals and primary metals to the processing industries like machinery.

The importance of primary industry will further decline and as we will see later, its form will undergo major changes.

In nominal terms, the share of secondary industry will drop as a whole because while its productivity will go up, the rise in prices will be relatively slower. The rise in the share of the machinery industry will be only modest. On the other hand, primary and tertiary industries will have bigger shares because of increases in relative prices. In particular, the share of the service industry will grow sharply from 33% in 1980 to some 50% in the year 2000.


[Changing Agriculture]

The development of Japanese agriculture over the past two decades has been characterized by the rapid growth of farming dependent on the use of facilities in contrast with the slump in farming primarily relying on the use of land. The main problems the industry faces today include improvements in productivity, reorganization of the production systems, and the need to ensure a secure food supply. The agricultural industry should develop in the following way over the coming years to overcome these problems (See Table 2-2-18).

In the first place, as to farming primarily dependent on the use of land, farmers are expected to become more competitive through an expansion of their business scale. A good many of them will be able to attain higher productivity in this way. Over the next 20 years, farming households will undergo dramatic generation changes, considering the old age of those who are now engaged in farming. An increasing amount of farm land will become fluid as farmers, unable to find their successors, are forced to either give up or trim the scale of their

## Table 2-2-18 The Supply and Demand of Principal Foodstuffs and the Outlook for Agriculture

|  | FY 1980 | FY 2000 |
|---|---|---|
| **Nutrition standards (per capita per day)** |  |  |
| Calorie intake (kilocalorie) | 2.512 | 2.500∿2.600 |
| Domestic calorie intake (kcal.) | 1.360 | Around 1.360 |
| Protein intake (g) | 80.7 | 88∿90 |
| Fat intake | 70.1 | 90∿93 |
| **Supply and demand of principal foodstuffs** |  |  |
| **Grains** |  |  |
| Consumption per capita per year (kg) | 113.9 | 88∿94 |
| Total demand (10,000 tons) | 3.695 | 4.000∿4.100 |
| Domestic demand (10,000 tons) | 1.075 | 1.100∿1.200 |
| Share of rice (10,000 tons) | 975 (bounty year crop: 1.112) | 850∿900 |
| **Meat (not including whale meat)** |  |  |
| Consumption per capita per year (kg) | 22.0 | 32∿35 |
| Total demand (10,000 tons) | 369 | 600∿640 |
| Domestic production (10,000 tons) | 298 | Around 490 |
| **Milk and dairy produce** |  |  |
| Consumption per capita per year (kg) | 62.2 | 84∿89 |
| Total demand (10,000 tons) | 756 | 1.100∿1.200 |
| Domestic production (10,000 tons) | 650 | 950∿1.000 |
| **Land utilization** |  |  |
| Total acreage (10,000 ha) | 564 | 630∿640 |
| Share of paddyfields (10,000 ha) | 235 | 150∿160 |
| Share of feed crops (10,000 ha) | 100 | 180∿200 |
| Acreage to be converted to other crops (10,000 ha) | 58 | Around 100 |
| Cultivated land space (10,000 ha) | 546 | 550∿560 |
| **Farming work force and farming households** |  |  |
| Farming population (10,000 people) | 2.137 | Around 1.420 |
| Share of those aged 60 or over (%) | 21.2 | " 36 |
| Those mainly engaged in farming (males) |  |  |
| (10,000 people) | 204 | " 115 |
| Share of those aged 60 or over (%) | 35.1 | " 53 |
| Number of farming households |  |  |
| (10,000 households) | 466 | " 350 |
| Share of households in which full-time male farmers are under 60 years of age (10,000 households) | 103 | " 40 |

**Notes:**

1. Based on "Food Supply-Demand Statistics," "Statistics on Arable Land and Crop-Planted Area" and "Agriculture and Forestry Census" of the Ministry of Agriculture, Forestry and Fisheries and the estimates of the Planning Bureau of the Economic Planning Agency.
2. Figures for the year 2000 are based on assumptions and ought to be interpreted with much latitude.

businesses. This should in turn enable other farmers to expand the scale of their businesses. If farm land can be put to concentrated use by core farmers and if pertinent price policies geared for such farmers are implemented, the number of agricultural businesses with 10 to 15 hectares of land for rice growing or 20 to 35 hectares of land for dairy farming will increase considerably. They should be able to attain price levels equal to those in many of the European Community nations. In that case, the number of core farming households in Japan is expected to decrease to some 400,000 from the present one million. As more consumers shift from rice to dairy products, farmers relying on land use will gradually change from "grain farming centered on rice growing" to "a combination of grain farming and dairy farming."

Now, as to farming dependent on the use of facilities, there will be further improvement in productivity as a result of enlarging the scale of business and technological innovations. Farmers of this type will be able to market their products not only at home but overseas as well.

[Materials Industry: From Adjustment to Rebirth]

Japan's materials industry grew fast in the 1960s, supported by an abundant supply of low-cost energy. Through an expansion of facilities, it became one of the most productive industries in the world. However, its growth has begun to slow down since the turn of the 1970s due in part to a lack of major technical innovations and also in part to the restraint on resources and energy supplies. Some sectors such as chemical and aluminum smelting have gradually lost their competitive edge, resulting in increasing imports.

This adjustment phase for the materials industry will continue throughout the 1980s. Problems for the industry will be all the greater because many of the large plants built in the 1960s will become obsolete and require replacement during this period.

However, if the new materials and new life science technologies being developed now can be put to practical use in the 1990s, the materials industry that used to depend on large-scale facilities and a massive consumption of energy may change into quite a different one. The processing and assembling industry, which is expected to grow in future, is in need of new materials better in quality or different in performance from conventional materials. On the basis of steel-making technology, the industry will develop new forms of business such as engineering and ocean development that can hardly be classified either as part of the conventional materials industry or the processing and assembling industry. In keeping with progress in "softwarization," industry of this type is expected to grow over the coming years.

[Growth Expected of Processing and Assembling Industry]

Japan's processing and assembling industry has developed rapidly, supported by the brisk domestic demand for durable consumer goods and capital goods. Today it is one of the most competitive industries in the world.

In the next two decades, further progress is to be made in technical innovations centering on electronics. Japan leads the world in this field and has the ability to put state-of-the-art technology to wide use in the processing and assembling industry. This means that the industry is assured of continued growth in the future. Industries supplying software are also expected to grow fast over the coming years, assisting the processing and assembling industry in developing sophisticated new products of higher added value.

In the field of consumer electronics and household appliances, such new products as information communication equipment and computers for home use will have a major impact on people's lifestyles. The information-related industry will develop to cover a wide range of fields. Integrated circuits will grow bigger in capacity. And the general machinery sector will become increasingly competitive through a wider application of electronics technology.

Efforts to develop new technology will be stepped up in the heavy-duty machinery sector. The automotive industry will retain its status as the key industry, but neither exports nor domestic demand will grow as fast as in the 1970s. The shipbuilding industry will try to branch out into new business fields in the face of growing competition from developing countries.

[Distribution Industry amid Matured Consumption Society]

For a long time, Japan's distribution industry was backward, largely made up of independent petty retailers and wholesalers. From the postwar rehabilitation years through the 1970s, this backward distribution system underwent a revolution in which the key role was played by newly organized supermarkets. Amid the growing

Westernization of lifestyles, the industry thus played a major role in ushering in an era of massive consumption.

However, in this matured consumption age when consumption tends to be more personal and diversified, those who play the major part in the distribution business also need to pluralize and diversify. It will become more and more important for distributors to get an accurate picture of ever-changing demand and feed it back to the producers.

In the retail sector, there will be an increase in the number of specialized and discount shops. The number of large-scale, integrated retail stores and stores located in suburban areas will increase. The distribution function will become increasingly systematic and sophisticated.

In the wholesale sector, the functions of information gathering and distributing goods in a way suitable to retailers will become more important, considering such factors as internationalization and the diversification of consumers' needs and personal preferences. But in the coming years the wholesale industry as a whole will not grow as fast as the retail industry, partly because the complicated distribution structure will continue to be reorganized and partly because business will slow down in the materials sector.

[Continued Growth of Service Industry]

The total share of tertiary industry in the economy has continued to grow both in terms of output value and number of employees. The growth of the service industry has been particularly remarkable since 1965. This growing share of the service industry is an inevitable result of increased income and matured consumption. This trend is expected to continue.

Given the diversification of needs and personal preferences, future growth is expected of two extremely different types of service industry — one in which labor is saved to the utmost and service rationalized as far as possible, and the other in which labor is offered intensively along with high-quality services.

As for services offered to individuals, the main growth areas will be sport, cultural, leisure-related and household care industries. As for services offered to offices, future growth is expected in the information processing and engineering industries. In the public service sector, the growth areas will be medicare, education and social welfare.

However, since productivity improvement is slow in the service industry, the gap is expected to widen between the growth in nominal and real terms.

[Change in Regional Economy]

Economic gaps between regions narrowed rapidly in the first half of the 1970s as a result of the government's policy of decentralizing industries. In recent years, however, the gaps have begun to widen again because of changes in the industrial structure and fiscal restraints. In future, economic development in the countryside may tend to be slower than in large cities for the following reasons: (1) Advanced industries such as electronics and fine chemicals which will lead industrial development over the coming years tend to site their facilities in big cities or nearby. (2) Production facilities are located mainly in the countryside, but employment in the production sector is expected to decrease as industry puts greater emphasis on software. On the other hand, the weight of the administrative sector in charge of research and development, product planning and business deals will grow and tend to be concentrated in large cities. (3) Growing internationalization and informationization will necessitate industry's executive functions to be concentrated more and more in large cities. (4) The local governments can no longer expect the lavish increase in fiscal transfers (such as tax subsidies and public works spending by the central government) that they used to enjoy in the years of high economic growth.

It will become necessary, therefore, to consider some effective measures to encourage the self-supported development of the regional economy.

It is also possible that the economic gaps between regional towns and remote areas will widen as the development of big regional towns and their vicinities is accelerated by the expansion of highway and air traffic networks. Furthermore, some industries may become stagnant, unable to cope with progress in the international division of labor. A regional economy highly dependent on such industry may then be hit by serious recession. There will be a need to revitalize this type of regional economy.

## (6)  Employment Structure

The labor market will change in many aspects over the next two decades, and employment structure in the year 2000 will be totally different from the one prevalent in the years of high economic growth.

Labor Supply to Slow Down after 1990]
The growth in Japan's labor force will be high at an annual rate of 1.0% in the 1980s, compared with 0.78% in the 1970s. But it is expected to slow down to a third (0.36%) in the 1990s.

This is because the drop in the birth rate after the first oil crisis will result in slower growth of the population of people aged 15 or over in the latter half of the 1990s. The growth in Japan's total population will remain little changed at an annual rate of 0.51% in the 1980s and 0.44% in the 1990s. But the growth in the population of people aged 15 or over will sharply decelerate from 1.17% in the 1980s to 0.51% in the 1990s.

As a result, Japan's labor force is expected to increase by 8.2 million over the next two decades from 57.1 million in 1980 to 65.3 million in the year 2000.

[Employment Structure in the Year 2000]
How will the employment structure change as a result of the change in the labor force? In Case I in the long-term multi-sectoral growth model, the employment structure will look like as indicated in Table 2-2-19. (The labor force estimates are based on the "Labor Force Survey." They cannot simply be compared with the labor force estimates based on the "National Census.")

According to the table, the number of people engaged in primary industry will drastically decrease despite the expansion in the scale of business. Its share in the total labor force will be almost halved.

Secondary industry will see a major increase in production output. But because of improved productivity, there will only be a modest increase in the number of workers, and a slight drop in their total share. One exception will be the machinery industry. The machinery industry expects some improvement in productivity, but the absolute volume of production will also increase significantly, so the number of workers will increase considerably as well.

## Table 2-2-19 The Outlook for the Employment Structure

| Industry | Number of employees by industry (10,000 people, %) | | | Average annual increase rate (%) | |
|---|---|---|---|---|---|
| | 1970 | 1980 | 2000 | 1970~1980 | 1980~2000 |
| Primary industry | 886 | 577 | 308 | -4.2 | -3.1 |
| | ( 17.4) | ( 10.4) | ( 4.9) | | |
| Secondary industry | 1,791 | 1,925 | 2,110 | 0.7 | 0.5 |
| | ( 35.2) | ( 34.8) | ( 33.3) | | |
| Mining and manufacturing | 1,397 | 1,377 | 1,420 | -0.1 | 0.2 |
| | ( 27.4) | ( 24.9) | ( 22.4) | | |
| Chemicals | 195 | 175 | 145 | -1.1 | -0.9 |
| | ( 3.8) | ( 3.2) | ( 2.3) | | |
| Primary metals | 82 | 67 | 54 | -2.0 | -1.1 |
| | ( 1.6) | ( 1.2) | ( 0.9) | | |
| Machinery | 527 | 538 | 893 | 0.2 | 2.6 |
| | ( 10.3) | ( 9.7) | ( 14.1) | | |
| Others | 593 | 597 | 328 | 0.1 | -3.0 |
| | ( 11.6) | ( 10.8) | ( 5.2) | | |
| Construction | 394 | 548 | 690 | 3.4 | 1.2 |
| | ( 7.7) | ( 9.9) | ( 10.9) | | |
| Tertiary industry | 2,409 | 3,019 | 3,912 | 2.3 | 1.3 |
| | ( 47.3) | ( 54.5) | ( 61.8) | | |
| Electricity, gas, water | 29 | 30 | 33 | 0.3 | 0.4 |
| | ( 0.6) | ( 0.5) | ( 0.5) | | |
| Finance, insurance, real estate | 132 | 191 | 241 | 3.8 | 1.2 |
| | ( 2.6) | ( 3.5) | ( 3.8) | | |
| Transportation, communication | 324 | 350 | 355 | 0.8 | 0.1 |
| | ( 6.4) | ( 6.3) | ( 5.6) | | |
| Services, etc. | 1,924 | 2,448 | 3,283 | 2.4 | 1.5 |
| | ( 37.8) | ( 44.2) | ( 52.0) | | |
| Total | 5,094 | 5,536 | 6,329 | 0.8 | 0.7 |
| | (100.0) | (100.0) | (100.0) | | |

**Notes:**
1. Based on "Census" and "Labor Force Survey" of the Statistics Bureau of the Prime Minister's Office and the estimates of the Planning Bureau of the Economic Planning Agency.
2. Totals for 1970 and 1980 include unclassified figures.
3. Estimates are based on "Labor Force Survey."
4. Labor force population is computed on the basis of "Census" while labor force supply and demand connot be simply compared.
5. Figures in parentheses denote shares in percentage.

The number of people engaged in tertiary industry will continue to increase. In particular, there will be a conspicuous increase in the number of persons engaged in the service industry where, despite the growing demand, productivity improvement will be harder to make. As a result, one out of every two people employed will be engaged in the service industry in the year 2000.

[Flow from "Upstream" to "Downstream" Industry]

We will now try to look into changes in employment structure in the context of the flow from "upstream" to "downstream" industries.

The process of producing raw materials and energy, processing them into products and bringing them to consumers is likened to a river. In this way, industries may be classified into three categories — agriculture, forestry and fishery; "upstream" industry (most manufacturing, construction, electricity, gas and water supply, etc.), and "downstream" industry (services, printing, publishing, etc.).

Progress in industrialization in postwar years began with the development of upstream industry centering on basic materials. Various types of downstream industry continued to grow on the basis of upstream industry. Their employment structure also changed accordingly. Between 1970 and 1980, the share of people engaged in agriculture, forestry and fishery dropped from 19.4% to 10.9% while that for upstream industry dropped from 34.3% to 33.9%. But the corresponding share for downstream industry rose from 46.3% to 55.0%

[Outlook for Category-Wise Employment Structure]

Table 2-2-20 shows how the employment structure will change for each of the three categories of industry over the next two decades.

The number of people engaged in upstream industry will grow at an annual rate of 0.3% from 1980 through the year 2000 to exceed one million, but their share in the total labor force will decline slightly. There will be more prominent changes in the sector-wise breakdown of workers. Those employed in the production of tools and equipment in, for instance, the machinery industry, and in construction will increase in number. But there will be drastic decreases in the number of those employed in the processing of agricultural and forestry products (such as the food industry) and in the processing of mineral products (such as the basic materials industry).

## Table 2-2-20 The Outlook for the Employment Structure by Category of Industry

**(1) Average annual increase rate** (In %)

| | 1970~1975 | 1975~1980 | 1980~2000 |
|---|---|---|---|
| Agriculture, forestry and fishery | -6.1 | -3.8 | -3.2 |
| Upstream industry | 0.5 | 0.6 | 0.3 |
| Downstream industry | 2.5 | 2.3 | 1.4 |

**(2) Increase or decrease** (In 10,000 people)

| | 1970~1980 | 1980~2000 |
|---|---|---|
| Agriculture, forestry and fishery | -403 | -292 |
| Upstream industry | 99 | 101 |
| Downstream industry | 648 | 1,010 |

**(3) Share** (In %)

| | 1970 | 1980 | 2000 |
|---|---|---|---|
| Agriculture, forestry and fishery | 19.4 | 10.9 | 4.9 |
| Upstream industry | 34.3 | 33.9 | 31.0 |
| Downstream industry | 46.3 | 55.0 | 63.6 |

Totals do not necessarily add up to 100% because they include figures that cannot be classified.

**Breakdown of upstream industry**

| | Increase or decrease between 1980 and 2000 (10,000 people) | Share in the year 2000 (%) |
|---|---|---|
| Agriculture and forestry processing | -136 | 2.0 |
| Apparel manufacturing | -55 | 2.1 |
| Minerals processing | -133 | 4.4 |
| Energy-related | -5 | 0.5 |
| Tool manufacturing | 374 | 12.9 |
| Construction | 56 | 9.2 |
| Upstream industry total | 101 | 31.0 |

**Breakdown of downstream industry**

| | Increase or decrease between 1980 and 2000 (10,000 people) | Share in the year 2000 (%) |
|---|---|---|
| Commerce | 271 | 20.4 |
| Transportation | 135 | 6.6 |
| Publication, communication, real estate, credit | 63 | 6.2 |
| Services offered to offices | 27 | 3.6 |
| Services offered to individuals | 193 | 11.3 |
| Social services | 321 | 15.6 |
| Downstream industry total | 1,010 | 63.6 |

**Note:** Based on "Census" of the Statistics Bureau of the Prime Minister's Office and the estimates of the Planning Bureau of the Economic Planning Agency.

The number of people engaged in downstream industry will increase at an annual rate of 1.4% to total 10.1 million in the year 2000. Their share in the total labor force will further rise to 63.6%. Much of the increase will come in the service industry, particularly in those sectors which provide individual and social services.

## (7) Trade and Overseas Investment

[Features of Japan's Trade Structure]
Several points characterize Japan's trade structure.

One is its vertical nature. The share of manufactured goods in total imports is low by international standards. In contrast, industrial products account for the bulk of Japanese exports. This may be attributed to these reasons: (1) Japan has traditionally lacked important natural resources, (2) unlike Western countries, Japan has had no industrially advanced countries nearby, (3) the Japanese population has been large enough to provide a good market for each domestic industry, and (4) historically, Japan has been in the process of catching up with Western countries in industrialization.

Another feature is that Japan's trade balances differ widely according to its trade partners. Japan is apt to suffer deficits in trade with developing countries (particularly countries possessing natural resources) and chalk up surpluses with industrially advanced countries. This is one of the basic factors that lie behind the occasional trade friction Japan has had with its Western trade partners.

[Moves Toward Horizontal Division of Labor]
However, Japan's trade structure will change considerably as the world economy and the Japanese industrial structure undergo major changes in the coming years.

The vertical trade structure will gradually change into one based on a horizontal division of labor, as the changes in industrial structure, reviewed earlier in this chapter, will lead to increased imports of manufactured goods.

[Growing Importance of Services Trade]
The services trade including finance, insurance, information and tourism will assume greater importance in overall trade just as the

service industry will claim a bigger share in the total economy. The World Bank estimates that the world's services trade will grow annually by 5% or over in real terms throughout the 1980s.

Japan's services economy ranks second after that of the United States. As it will continue growing, Japan will gain an increasingly big share of the international services market.

Particularly rapid growth is expected in the fields of computer data processing and information service.

[Increase in Direct Investment]
There will be a steady increase in the volume of Japan's direct investment overseas. Japanese investment in the past has been directed mainly to developing countries for the purpose of developing natural resources and using cheaper local labor.

Japan's investment overseas is expected to continue growing for these reasons: (1) Japan's technical and managerial capacity has grown competitive internationally, (2) it has become increasingly difficult to merely seek an expansion of exports, and (3) production costs in Japan are becoming relatively high, mainly pushed up by the increase in wage costs.

While investment of the conventional type in developing countries will actively continue, there will be an increase in the number of large-scale investment projects in high-tech fields in industrially advanced countries. In the materials industry, re-arranging production facilities in an international perspective will become a major problem, and a number of firms in the industry will positively choose to invest outside Japan.

## 3. People's Lifestyles

### (1) Changes in Sense of Value and Consciousness

[Changes in Sense of Value and Consciousness in Recent Years and Future Trends]
People's sense of value and consciousness have changed much in recent years. Some of the new general trends include a stronger desire for varied moral and cultural satisfaction, a desire to seek new human relationships in regional communities and a growing yearning for

nature, switching from a life devoted to business to a life in which business and personal or household affairs can be compatible, the growth of middle-class consciousness, and a new consciousness of the roles played by men and women.

These changes may be attributed to (1) the loss of traditional regional connections and the growth of an urban way of thinking, prompted by the changes in employment structure as exemplified by the decline of primary industry and the rise of secondary and tertiary industries, and by the progress of urbanization, (2) the improvement in income standards and the increase in leisure time that have encouraged people to seek greater affluence in life, and (3) longer academic careers that have prompted people to have stronger aspirations for self-realization.

These new trends, particularly the desire for moral and cultural satisfaction and aspirations for self-realization, are expected to continue.

Diversification of sense of value will also progress as people come to prize a society in which they can freely think and behave in their own way.

[Aspects That Will Not Change]

Amid these changes in people's lifestyles, there will be something that will fundamentally not change. Historically, Japan has been a homogenous farming society in which harmony rather than confrontation is valued and group human relations rather than individuals are given greater consideration in resolving problems. High regard for harmony seems to underlie the principle the Japanese abide by in trying to settle their problems.

This principle has been retained in the Japanese economic system, despite the rise of Western individualism and rationalism in postwar years and the progress of industrialization and urbanization in more recent years. It has given rise to dynamic competition based on the unity, reliance and vitality of Japanese society, contributing a great deal toward Japan's fast economic growth.

These social and cultural characteristics will continue to govern the behavior of the Japanese people and provide the Japanese economy with its source of vitality.

## (2)  Outlook for People's Lifestyles

[Important Family and Community Roles]
The general trend towards a smaller household will continue with
a resultant increase in the number of households made up of only an
aged couple or an aged single person (particularly female).

At present, about 70% of those aged 65 or over live with married
sons or daughters. An estimate based on the assumption that the
changes in the ratio of reversion to household in recent years will
continue shows that this rate will go down in future. However, there are
also some factors that will increase this rate. One, for example, is the
trend towards settling in regions under such conditions as an increase
in the ratio of eldest son or daughter to the total number of children.
Depending on future economic developments and changes in the
people's way of thinking, the ratio of aged people living with sons or
daughters may increase over the coming years. The stronger "live
together" trend in Japan is likely to remain basically unchanged. Even
if they choose to live separately, more parents and children will decide
to live next to each other or live in the same area.

Meanwhile, amid the diversifying sense of values, increasing
volume of free time and aging population, greater importance will come
to be attached to the family or community life. The roles played by the
family or community will come to be reviewed in various fields such as
family education (training of children and transmission from
generation to generation), mutual assistance, leisure activity and
community activity (hobbies, culture, learning and volunteer activities,
etc.).

Towards the end of the current century, Japan will have changed
into a society in which the family and community assume increasingly
important functions.

[Formation of Life Cycle Fit for 80-Year Life Span]
Every person has their own important and memorable occasions
during their lifetime, such as entering school, graduation, finding
employment, marriage, the birth of the first baby, marriage of the last
child, retirement, etc. All these combine to form their life cycle.

As Figure 2-3-1 indicates, typical life cycles in Japan have changed
dramatically since the Meiji Era. The most outstanding change has

been the expansion of the average life span to 80 years. This simply means that one has a long life after retirement. Another major change has been a decrease in the number of children, which means a shorter period of time required for bringing them up. As a result, people can expect to gain a period of time after bringing up children equal to a third of their lifetime. Changes in life cycle have been particularly drastic for women.

These changes along with the increase in number of people who will actually go through such a stage in life because of aging of the population will have a great impact on the national economy and various aspects of living in future towards the 21st century. For example, free time will increase and more people will come into the labor market or take part more frequently in social and community affairs. On the other hand, efforts will be made to set up a new social system geared to these changes. Such efforts are important and necessary for bettering the quality of life and maintaining the vitality of society.

[Steady Increase in Free Time]

An average person's living time can be broken down into (1) vital time for sleeping, eating and doing personal things, (2) restrained time for doing business, studying at school, doing household work or commuting, and (3) free time for keeping company, taking rest or enjoying leisure activity. The distribution of time has changed with the change of the times.

There has been little change in the length of "vital time" in recent years. However, the length of "free time" has drastically increased as that of "restrained time" decreases mainly because of shortening work hours. In future, the ratio of "free time" to total living time will continue to increase steadily, as people make greater efforts to find more leisure time, with work hours shortening due to the introduction of a five-day week and more housewife work services being assigned to external markets. By the year 2000, a five-day week will be the general practice in Japan and people will be having longer summer holidays.

On the other hand, as the average life span lengthens and the average number of children decreases, people will have more time after retirement or bringing-up their children. As a result of these changes in life style, the length of free time during a lifetime is increasing. Further-

## Fig. 2-3-1   The Changes in Life Cycle by Generation

**(1)   Changes in Period of Child Rearing**

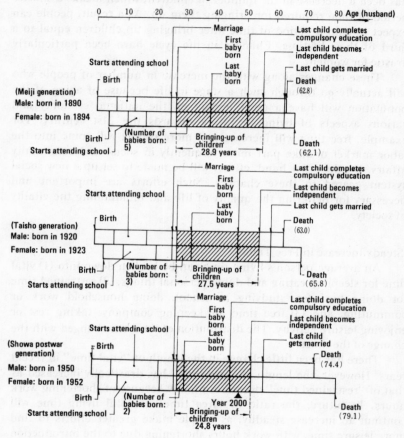

**Notes:**
1. **Sources:** Statistics and Information Department of the Ministry of Health and Welfare "Vital Statistics," "Life Table" and the Institute of Population Problems, the Ministry of Health and Welfare "Survey on Childbirth."
2. The last child is considered to be independent upon graduation from university (now defunct middle school for Meiji generation).

## (2)  Changes in Period after Last Child Goes Independent

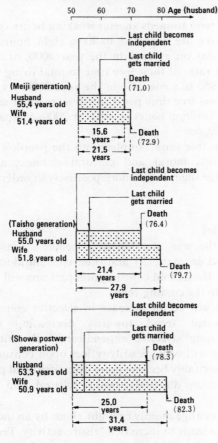

50    60    70    80 **Age (husband)**

Last child becomes independent

Last child gets married

Death (71.0)

(Meiji generation)
Husband
55.4 years old
Wife
51.4 years old

15.6 years — Death (72.9)

21.5 years

Last child becomes independent

Last child gets married

Death (76.4)

(Taisho generation)
Husband
55.0 years old
Wife
51.8 years old

21.4 years

Death (79.7)

27.9 years

Last child becomes independent

Last child gets married

Death (78.3)

(Showa postwar generation)
Husband
53.3 years old
Wife
50.9 years old

25.0 years

Death (82.3)

31.4 years

3.  The death year in (1) was computed from the average life span at the time when the last child went independent.

4.  The death year in (2) was computed from the average life span at the time when the last child went independent.

more, as the number of people who have more free time will increase considerably within the aging process, it is certain that the distribution of total time for Japanese as a whole will move towards a double or triple increase in free time.

Provided that the trend towards shorter working hours continues, Japanese aged 10 or over are expected to have eight hours and 10 minutes of free time a day on average in the year 2000, or one hour more than in 1980. The ratio of their free time to total living time will increase from 30% in 1980 to some 34% in the year 2000. As a result, the Japanese people's total free time per day will increase at an annual rate of 1.3% to reach 930 million hours in the year 2000, compared with 700 million hours in 1980.

Such an increase in free time, coupled with the people's growing desire for more comfort, moral and cultural richness and self-realization, will encourage them to act more positively in order to enjoy leisure activity.


[Changing Consumer Life]
Since the end of the war, the Japanese people's consumption standards have improved dramatically and their consumption pattern has changed drastically. Household consumption patterns will undergo equally drastic changes in the coming years.

One future change will be an increase in selective consumption expenditure. The present trend towards decreasing essential expenditure and increasing selective expenditure will continue. A diversified sense of value will come readily reflect upon consumer life. And consumption will inevitably become more diversified and personal, with an increasing portion directed toward cultural and creative purposes.

Another will be the change mainly brought about by an increase in free time. More free time leads to increased leisure activity. People will come to spend more of their time on something active and self-realizing such as playing sport and hobbies rather than on passive things such as taking rest.

A major change will also come from an increase in the number of aged people. Old generations have more money and time to spend and are keen on health. The increase in the number of such people will lead to greater demand for special goods of high quality and goods aimed at maintaining their health.

Another important change will be caused by factors attributable to the suppliers of goods. For example, technical progress in electronics and mechatronics will affect daily consumer life in various ways. Just exactly how is hard to foresee. However, the introduction of personal computers, and two-way television and facsimile systems could bring about major changes to the pattern of shopping or commuting. The arrival of new electronic products and the increase in the number of young generations familiar with electronic equipment (electronic generations) could make these changes far-reaching.

A change will occur in the way services are offered. As a result of an increase in the number of family restaurants, nursery schools and baby sitters, catering, nursing and other domestic services will come to be assigned to external markets. On the other hand, the growing "do it yourself" tendency and technical innovations will turn more services provided externally into domestic affairs.

[Consumption Structure in the Year 2000]

With these changes taken into account, consumption structure (based on real value at the 1975 price) in the year 2000 will look like that given in Table 2-3-2.

It is clear from this table that the share of food expenses will decrease significantly (though there will be an increase in "eating out expenses"), that there will be a modest decrease in clothing expenses, that housing expenses will increase slightly reflecting the people's desire for a better quality of residence, and that the share of miscellaneous expenses, mainly cultural and entertainment expenses and medicare expenses, will increase drastically, due mainly to an increase in the number of old generations.

[Lifetime Education and Learning]

The most outstanding change in education in the postwar years has been the rapid increase in the ratio of people going on to senior high school or college. Japan now ranks second after the United States in the ratio of people advancing to university (including two-year colleges). The ratio in Japan stood at 36.9% in 1980.

With this ratio likely to remain virtually unchanged over the coming years, the share of learned persons in the population of people

## Table 2-3-2    Changes in Consumption Structure

(In %)

| Year | 1963 | 1970 | 1980 | 2000 |
|---|---|---|---|---|
| Consumption structure (share in real consumption expenditure) | | | | |
| Food expenses | 39.7 | 33.6 | 29.3 | 22.2 |
| Dwelling expenses | 9.8 | 10.6 | 9.5 | 11.1 |
| Lighting and heating expenses | 3.1 | 3.4 | 3.9 | 3.5 |
| Clothing expenses | 12.5 | 11.3 | 9.3 | 8.3 |
| Miscellaneous expenses | 35.0 | 41.1 | 48.1 | 54.9 |
| Health and medicare | 1.4 | 2.0 | 2.6 | 3.4 |
| Traffic, communication, auto-related expenses | 2.8 | 4.9 | 7.9 | 8.3 |
| Education, stationery, culture and entertainment | 11.9 | 11.2 | 11.3 | 10.0 |
| Others | 18.9 | 23.0 | 26.3 | 33.2 |

**Notes:**
1. Based on "Family Income and Expenditure Survey" and "Consumer Price Index" of the Statistics Bureau of the Prime Minister's Office and the estimates by the Planning Bureau of the Economic Planning Agency.
2. Also based on workers' households as covered in "Family Income and Expenditure Survey."
3. "Others" include hair-dressing, sanitation, tobacco, remittances, charges, casualty insurance premiums, social expenses, etc.

aged 20 or over will rise to around 25% in the year 2000 from 7% in 1960 and 16% in 1980.

In recent years, an increasing number of people have been prepared to learn throughout their lifetime. This trend is likely to gain momentum in future. More adults are now eager to continue opportunities for education and learning. More people now feel the necessity to update their knowledge and techniques especially in connection with their professional life. And there are more opportunities to learn outside school. In addition to the development of the mass media, more cultural centers and academic seminars are open to the public.

Future lifetime education and learning should be designed to retrain professional people in new social changes and technology, train women to help them resume a career after bringing up their children, help middle-aged people to re-develop their abilities, and help people change their occupation. It should also be aimed at providing women and aged people without careers with opportunities to learn something that would give them a sense of accomplishment and participation.

(3)   Changes in Residential Space

Over the next two decades, there will be various changes in residential space as a result of progressive urbanization and the people's growing desire for improvement in the living environment.

[Urbanization to Become National Trend]
Urbanization has progressed rapidly in Japan since the end of the war. In view of the increasing share of tertiary industry and the growing share of white collar workers, an urbanized life style will become a nationwide trend and progress further.

In large cities and adjacent areas, urbanization caused by social population increases has already passed its peak. But in these areas there will be a major natural increase in population. So the growth of nuclear cities and satellite cities around big cities is expected to promote regional urbanization.

In the countryside, urbanization is likely to progress fairly fast as a result of the development of traffic and communication facilities and an increase in the number of people who choose to settle there. Population and facilities will continue to concentrate particularly in major local cities such as prefectural capitals.

[Qualitative Change and Diversification of Desires Concerning Living Environment and Residence]
As people earn higher incomes, have more free time, study longer and grow older, their desires concerning the living environment will become stronger and diverse. They will also come to care not only for hardware elements such as facilities but software elements like nature,

culture and the beauty of their living environment, and become more willing to participate in the formation of the environment in which they live.

The quantitative demand for houses is not likely to grow much in the future, but requirements for houses of better quality will become increasingly strong. Parents and children are expected to have various options about the way they live; some deciding to live together, others choosing to live separately in the same premises, and still others opting to live seperately in the same area. More people will seek qualitative improvement in their residences by building extensions onto their old houses, renewing old equipment and facilities or trading in old houses for new ones.

# Chapter 3　Three Trends and a Basic Strategy For the 21st Century

Japanese economic society towards the 21st century will be struck by waves of diversified change. To put them in order of intensity, the waves will be "internationalization," "an aging society," and "maturity." In this chapter, we will think about a basic strategy necessary to conquer the problems confronting us amidst such changes.

## Section 1　The Internationalization of Economic Society and Accommodation on a Global Scale

Japan has up till now achieved its development as a member of the world. There is no other way for Japan to survive in future except to continue maintaining peaceful and steady relations with the rest of the world. Internationalization will further progess and Japan's international obligations will increase. Against such a background, it is believed that how Japan behaves will become significantly important.

### 1.　The Progress in Internationalization and Enlargement of International Duty

(1)　Progress in Internationalization

[Currents of Internationalization]
The Internationalization of various fields has taken place in the past. It is assumed that in a long-term perspective the trend toward internationalization will further accelerate in force. The mode of internationalization is likely to be diversified and international exchange will become common on a daily basis. It will become necessary for us to look at all problems from an international point of view.

Future progress in internationalization will not simply expand in quantity but will be different in quality from the advance made thus far. If anything, internationalization so far has mainly been in the economic field, an area which is rather easy to cope with.

However, as the level of internationalization deepens in future, the trend will further advance in multilateral fields, including areas related to Japan's economic society. Therefore, we must be prepared to see the emergence of a situation in which we will be forced to cope with various difficulties.

In the following, we will look at the progress in internationalization of four different fields, including (a) the commodities and service trade; (b) capital transfers; (c) enterprise management; and (d) information and culture.

a.   Progress in the Commodities and Service Trade

As the international division of labor moves ahead through trade, it is presumed that Japan will strengthen its ties with the world economy also through trade. Changes in relations involving the international division of labor will bring about industrial coordination in various countries. If such industrial coordination fails to make smooth progress, there will be trade friction.

Also, it is assumed that the following developments may accompany any future industrial coordination through trade:

[Trade Friction with Advanced Countries]
During its stage of catching up with the United States and advanced European countries, Japan went ahead with improvement of its industrial structure and expanded exports of its industrial products. In the process, however, trade friction came about with the target items changing from textiles to steel and automobiles. Such disputes resulted from the lack of smooth progress in industrial coordination in advanced countries receiving Japanese exports.

From now on, Japan is expected to increase its production and exports centering around its processing and assembly industry. There is a possibility of new trade friction occurring because the Japanese attempt to seek the growth of industry with high added value is a common direction pursued by the United States and other industrially advanced nations.

[Domestic Industrial Coordination]

On the other hand, the domestic Japanese basic material industry will have to go ahead with industrial coordination. From the principle of relative predominance, the processing and assembly industry's strong international competitiveness will serve as a primary factor in forcing the basic materials industry to adjust itself. Also, the progress of industrialization in developing countries, increases in energy prices and the resource exporting nations' inclination towards high added value will form the main causes of disadvantage for the Japanese basic materials industry.

In the midst of the large tendency towards internationalization, Japan must move ahead with industrial coordination. In such an event, the basic materials industry will exert a relatively large degree of influence on other industries through its changes. Regionally, there will be many cases of the formation of so-called "castle towns of enterprises." There will also be difficulties seriously affecting the regional economy.

b.  The Internationalization of Capital Transfers

Internationalization is expected to move forward not only in "materials" but also in "money."

[Expansion of Import and Export Capital]

It is expected that both Japanese import and export capital will increase in future.

Increases in export capital are expected because of (1) an expansion of direct investment (refer to Chapter 2 Section 2 (7)), (2) rises in indirect investment resulting from internationalization of the use of funds, and (3) increases in overseas loans such as yen credits along with the promotion of economic cooperation.

On the other hand, import capital is likely to continue expanding against the background of rises in indirect investment in Japan due to overseas countries' appreciation of the Japanese economy's good performance, and increases in direct investment in Japan in connection with the internationalization of the Japanese economy.

[Internationalization of the Yen]

The importance of the yen as an international currency will grow further, and the yen's trend toward internationalization will move ahead.

The internationalization of the yen is expected to make rapid progress in connection with the internationalization of the Japanese economy as a whole, particularly with rises in the relative importance of international monetary transactions, and also with the rise in Japan's relative position in the world economy.

The internationalization of the yen thus far has merely centered on the tendency to regard it in terms of reserve assets. The yen has not been fully used as either an indicator currency or a currency for the settlement of accounts. However, in future, a balanced internationalization of the yen will make progress as the domestic short-term monetary market becomes complete and opportunities for the use and procurement of the yen as short-term capital by non-residents expand. Such a development will trigger demand for the Japanese currency as a means for transactions and the settlement of accounts.

The progress in internationalization of the currency and monetary fields as stated above will function as an important element for reforming the domestic monetary system. And, the Japanese monetary market will upgrade its international role.


c. The Internationalization of Enterprises

[Progress in the Internationalization of Enterprises]

With the saturation of the domestic market under the medium growth of the economy, trade friction with the United States and European countries and the promotion of development and imports of energy resources in the background, the internationalization of enterprise activities including production in overseas countries in future will advance further. The substance of such activities also will be diversified. In the midst of all this, multinational corporations may make their debut. On the other hand, internationalization of the domestic market will move forward and foreign enterprises will become active in Japan.

Pursuant to such large scale international business developments, increases in management risk, particularly country risk and project risk, will be expected.

[Management Control System to Be Pressed for Changes]
Under the further internationalization of enterprises, the existing management control system is likely to be forced to make new accommodations.

The accommodation of Japanese enterprises to past internationalization has systematically been divided into two parts — domestic and overseas — centering on the system of controlling local overseas corporate firms by dispatching management personnel abroad. However, in establishing genuine overseas business activities, it will be necessary for Japanese enterprises to combine the domestic and overseas sectors into one organic sector and work out an equal management strategy. On that occasion, it will be necessary for them to make good use of non-Japanese staff personnel for the multinationalization of personnel.

d. The Internationalization of Information and Culture

[Further Progress in the Internationalization of Information and Culture]
Progress in the means of transportation and communications has so far brought about active international exchanges of information and personnel, and has led the earth to become smaller and move homogeneous.

The internationalization of information and culture will make further progress in future with the support of the development of electronic technology.

[The Need for Mutual Understanding Will Rise]
Even though international exchanges may fast increase on the surface, essentially it takes time to understand people of different races and their culture. Under such circumstances, progress in internationalization of the economic side alone without any progress in mutual understanding, including the cultural field, may exacerbate economic friction.

However, it is possible to achieve balanced progress in both economic and cultural internationalization if efforts are made to promote international exchanges at diversified levels and deepen mutual understanding. Such endeavors will become a turning point for new cultural development of the Japanese culture which, historically speaking, has formed itself through contact with different kinds of culture and maintained harmony with them.

(2)    The Need for the Positive Accommodation of Internationalization

In the midst of changes in the international environment around Japan, it will become inevitable for this nation to cope more positively with internationalization than before and intensify the degree of its international contributions. This is because the world economy and Japan's relations with it will move in the following direction:

[A Confused World Economy]
First, the world economy is faced with many problems and is in need of cooperative efforts between Japan and other countries.

As mentioned in Chapter 2, the world economy is confronted with a number of issues, including the decline in its vigor, which must be resolved. The decade of the 1980s can be positioned as a period of coordination for settling such problems. Also, the completion of a framework for settlement of the issues cannot be expected as in the past with the existence of such an overwhelmingly large country as the United States. Cooperative efforts under the banner of multipolarization will be requested. In this situation, Japan will be asked to make positive contributions in a direction to be stated in Section 2.

[The Significance of the World Economy for Japan]
Second, Japan can remain in existence only in the family of world nations. As in the past, Japan can expect to achieve development only by maintaining relations of stability and mutual dependence with a world economy rich in vitality.

It is important for Japan to positively respond to internationalization for the sake of maintaining its security. Japan relies on overseas countries for a variety of main commodities such as natural resources, energy and foodstuffs. It cannot isolate itself from international society and seek self-sufficient national security. Japan must try to maintain its security under international mutual dependence. Towards that goal, it must increase the degree of its international contributions, further diversify a network of international mutual reliance not only in the economic field but also in the political, diplomatic, cultural and social fields, and should become an indispensable organizational element of international society by deepening such a network.

Japan is a country which can induce the most significant merit from a steadily developed world economy. It is because of this that the world economy is very significant for Japan and that the need for its positive accommodation of internationalization is high.

[Intensified Japanese Influence]

Third, as Japan has enhanced its position in the world economy, its degree of influence on the world economy has also increased. Japan has the power to contribute significantly to the stability and vitality of the world from now on in a leading role among industrially advanced nations.

Also, as Japan gains further status in the world economy, more than ever, it cannot divorce itself from the world in achieving its economic growth. Amidst a stagnant world economy, there will be increased economic friction if Japan alone tries to seek further economic growth. Economic growth itself will face limits. There must be international harmony in the form of economic growth as well.

Although Japan has gained a higher position in the world economy, there is a limit to its power. In its leading role in a multipolarized world, where attempts are made to settle problems cooperatively, Japan must set its goal in a direction towards a more positive role than before.

## 2. Basic Strategy for Internationalization

(1) Revitalization of the World Economy

The first basic strategy for various problems emerging in the internationalization process is to render positive service towards revitalizing the world economy.

Many of the problems confronting the world economy today are due to the decline in its vitality and a zero sum situation. Therefore, efforts must be made to try to revitalize the world economy and bring about a plus sum situation.

a. Reconstruction of the World Economic Order

It may be said that the international economic structure at present is not offering enough of a framework to resolve the various problems confronting the world economy in trade and international monetary affairs. In order to seek steady development of the world economy towards the 21st century, it is necessary to establish a new international economic system and international rules.

[Preservation of the Foundation for the Free Trade System]

What is important for the reconstruction of the international economic order is to establish relations of steady mutual dependence based on free trade.

If each nation in the world merely becomes conscious of the negative aspects of mutual reliance and copes in a short-term manner, there will be an expansion of protectionism and isolationism with the world economy heading for a scale-down equilibrium.

Table 3-1-1 shows the effects of a 10% discriminatory increase in dollar prices of Japanese commodities exported to the United States and European nations, based on a world economic model worked out by the Economic Research Institute of the Economic Planning Agency in order to study the effect of protectionist measures on the world economy.

According to the results of this simulation, protectionist measures will bring about a trifling short-term increase in income and a positive effect on employment in some countries, but will worsen stagflation of the world economy over medium and long periods.

The preservation of the free trade system does not only bring large profits to industrially advanced countries but is also very significant for developing nations about to face a period of economic growth. A wide opening of the markets of industrially advanced nations to both industrial and other products from the developing countries will sustain

**Table 3-1-1 The Effects of Imports Restriction Measures Against Japan as Seen in the World Economic Model**

(In %)

|  | 1st year | 2nd year | 3rd year | 4th year |
|---|---|---|---|---|
| **GNP in real terms** | | | | |
| U.S. | −0.22 | −0.60 | −0.80 | −0.77 |
| Britain | −0.06 | −0.34 | −0.42 | −0.44 |
| France | 0.01 | −0.12 | −0.36 | −0.54 |
| West Germany | 0.01 | −0.21 | −0.45 | −0.72 |
| Japan | −0.38 | −0.90 | −1.11 | −1.08 |
| **Consumption deflator** | | | | |
| U.S. | 0.26 | 0.32 | 0.30 | 0.22 |
| Britain | 0.12 | 0.27 | 0.12 | −0.03 |
| France | 0.06 | 0.10 | 0.11 | 0.11 |
| West Germany | 0.02 | 0.05 | 0.05 | −0.01 |
| Japan | 0.24 | 0.90 | 1.91 | 3.13 |
| **World trade in real terms** | −0.18 | −0.67 | −1.01 | −1.22 |
| **GNP total for nine countries** | −0.15 | −0.47 | −0.67 | −0.73 |

**Notes:**
1. Figures show the ratio of separation as against the standard key which shows the effect of a 10% discriminatory price increase in Japanese export prices from the 1975 level for goods bound for the U.S., Britain, France, West Germany, Italy, Canada and other Western European nations.
2. Domestic demand deflator was used to show the consumption deflator in France.
3. The nine nations are the U.S., Britain, France, West Germany, Italy, Canada, Japan, Australia, and the Republic of Korea.

these countries, industrialization and autonomous development. However, under free trade, it is the principle of relative international ascendancy that functions, and changes may come forth in the dynamic industrial and trade structures of various countries. If they move ahead at a rapid pace, there will be international friction. Therefore, it is necessary for both exporting and importing countries to take into account the time necessary for coordination and to accommodate each other in a spirit of cooperation in order to maintain the framework of free trade as a whole.

In recent years, there has been a rising trend towards protectionism against the background of a stagnant world economy and increased difficulty in achieving industrial coordination. Moves for import restrictions have also been seen. It is necessary for Japan to take note of the above and become a forerunner in making efforts to preserve the free trade system.

[Reconstruction of the International Economic System]

The following can be considered as a concrete direction towards reconstruction of the international economic system for establishing steady mutual relations:

First, GATT's function should be further strengthened. To this end, attempts should be made to activate GATT by the systematic reinforcement of conditions for invoking safe-guards (for example, completion of a multiple supervision structure) and cooperation in its management. Trade friction should be settled at a multilateral forum. It is also necessary to create an international consensus on the limitation of government intervention. Also, there is a need to prepare a liberalization code for the service trade, which is expected to increase its importance in future.

Second, it is necessary to draw up common international rules comparable to GATT in order to deal with direct investment.

Third, in the international monetary field, it is necessary to have cooperation among various countries on economic policies so that there will be a steady operation of exchange fluctuations. Also, the role of international reserve assets such as the SDR ought to be strengthened as well as that of the IMF.

Fourth, it is necessary for industrially advanced nations and developing countries to deepen policy dialogue in the field of economic cooperation.

b. The Practical Use of Japanese Economic Vitality

It is possible for Japan to sustain a relatively vital economic performance among the developed nations as long as it does not make any mistake in its future measures. It is also necessary for Japan to bind this economic vitality to the activation of the world economy.

[The Realization of Medium Growth Centering on Domestic Demand]
First, Japan must conduct rational economic management and try to accomplish economic growth centering on domestic demand.

As seen in Chapter 2, it is possible for Japan to continue registering economic growth slightly higher (medium growth) than other advanced countries during the period going into the 21st century. This is considered desirable not only for Japan but for the world economy as well.

In the midst of world economic stagnation, Japan could contribute to the development of the world economy by sustaining the policy of medium growth in its economy centering on domestic demand because Japan accounts for 10% of the entire world economy. Also, the growth of Japan, which provides a big market for developing nations, will help increase shipments of primary and industrial products from developing nations which are struck by economic difficulties. It will become effective economic cooperation when autonomous development of such developing countries is brought about.

[Expansion of Industrial Cooperation]

Second, industrial cooperation through technical cooperation and direct investment should be promoted.

It is necessary for Japan to transfer to overseas countries in the form of technical cooperation the results of technical innovation likely to develop here in future. Japan should also make direct investments to seek improvements in productivity, if it is to make use of the vitality of private enterprise — the driving force of the Japanese economy — to revitalize the world economy.

c.   Strengthening Economic Solidarity in Pacific Region

In the Pacific region surrounding Japan, there are many diverse countries possessed with the hidden possibility of developing greatly towards the 21st century by assisting each other. If economic solidarity progresses in this area and the region's potential power for growth is fully demonstrated, it is possible that the Pacific region will become the nucleus of revitalization of the world economy.

[Pacific Area Has Great Potential]

Many different countries exist in the Pacific zone, including two major industrialized countries — Japan and the United States — as well as new emerging industrialized nations, the Republic of Korea and Mexico, semi-emerging industrialized countries in ASEAN, and advanced resource affluent countries like Canada and Australia. They all maintain the possibility of establishing deep mutual relations, and are expected to achieve the highest growth in the world economy as they move towards the 21st century.

They have generally continued to record high economic growth compared with other regions by deepening their relations of mutual dependence. Also, Japan's economic relations with various Pacific region countries hold significant mutual importance.

[The Strengthening of Economic Solidarity]

Thus, it is both significant for Japan as well as world economy to maintain strong economic ties and strengthen economic solidarity with the Pacific zone which has the potential for major development, to fully demonstrate the region's potential power.

It is necessary for Japan to make good use of its economic power and its experience gained from economic development. It should base its policy on offering positive contributions to the economic development of the Pacific area and should try to extend cooperation from all sides for strengthening solidarity with the region.

Of course, any economic solidarity in the Pacific zone should not move towards exclusive regionalism. Any effort towards that goal must be directed at the establishment of relations of flexible solidarity open to the world.

(2) Formation of Open Economic Society

It is necessary for Japan to form an internationally open economic society in order to respond to increases in its international obligations, survive in the world and cope positively with progress in internationalization.

a. Open Market and Implementation of Smooth Industrial Coordination

[Promotion of Open Market]
Japan has rapidly opened its market since 1960 with the implementation of measures for liberalizing trade and reducing tariffs. It can be said that at present Japan is generally on a par with other advanced countries in the number of items on the residual import restriction list and tariffs, or is even more generous than them in opening its market to foreign goods. However, in reality, the ratio of imports to domestic consumption is lower than in the United States and European countries in some aspects, and the degree of the horizontal division of labor in industry is still low.

Japan must press ahead with further efforts to open up its market more than now and promote the horizontal division of labor in industry because it is highly dependent on the world and is receiving considerable benefits from free trade.

[Implementation of Smooth Industrial Coordination]
Japan could play the role of checking the trend towards protectionist trade and ease trade friction involving Japanese exports by opening its market wider in responding positively to progress in internationalization, going ahead with the horizontal division of labor within industry and taking the initiative in tackling the maintenance of the free trade system. Such endeavors also will help advance the efficiency of the Japanese economy in macro terms.

However, in micro terms, it is conceivable that there will be industries which plunge into difficulty along with the progress in the opening of the Japanese market and changes in trade structure. In such a situation, the aforementioned alterations could be hindered if Japan fails to make progress in smooth industrial coordination. Moves towards protectionist trade also might emerge within the country.

Therefore, it is necessary for this country to carry out smooth industrial coordination through the maintenance and strengthening of market functions and smooth adjustment of the demand and supply of the labor force in order to form and maintain economic vitality (mentioned later). It must also not lose the power to cope with change.

b. Completion of the Domestic System in Answer to the Internationalization Trend

There are still many aspects remaining in the Japanese social framework which do not necessarily presuppose progress in internationalization. The Japanese government, corporations and society may be pressed to deepen their perception of the internationalization trend, complete a domestic system to meet such a tendency and revise their consciousness in answer to internationalization, which is expected to accelerate in future.

[Economic Management under Internationalization]

First, the government must shift the management of its economic policy to cope with internationalization.

More specifically, it is necessary for the government to continue placing emphasis on overseas economic areas in its economic policy, make the substance of its economic policy easy to understand for overseas countries, make it clear on relations between those areas entrusted to the private sector and the role and duty of the government, and substantiate Japan's basic attitude towards and public relations activities concerning Japan's economic policy. It must also make unceasing efforts to gain the understanding and support of various foreign countries.

Also, it is necessary for Japan to take note of the considerable influence its behavior will have on the world economy and manage its economic policy by always bearing the "steady development of the world economy" in mind.

[The Need for Social Accommodation]

Socially, Japan will probably have to seriously grapple with the task of accommodating internationalization.

However, Japan is an extremely homogenous society arising from its own geographical conditions and historical background. It is important for Japanese people of all social standings to pay full attention to the difficulties and friction which may accompany internationalization, and fundamentally equip themselves with a sense of international being to establish a society capable of coping with internationalization.

For that purpose, efforts must be made to further promote the internationalization of universities and research organs, school education must be fulfilled from an international point of view, an educational environment for both young Japanese abroad and returnees should be provided.

International exchange in corporate activities and personnel exchange on a regional basis are likely to deepen. Under such circumstances, it is necessary for center cities in blocs to strengthen their international functions and realize regional international exchange without going through metropolises.

Also, it is necessary for Japan to march forward with personnel exchanges in order to open itself internationally both in the economic and social fields. Japan needs to take a renewed look at this matter from an international perspective.

## (3) Accommodating Global Problems

It is very important for Japan to accommodate various global-scale problems leading up to the 21st century, including the North-South issue, foodstuffs and the environment. Japan must make positive contributions to the settlement of these problems.

### a. Maintenance of Peaceful International Environment

Since World War II, the world has generally made progress in peace without large-scale conflicts, although there have been regional wars. The maintenance of such a peaceful environment is a major precondition to the settlement of various problems on a global scale.

However, a peaceful environment alone will not resolve the problems. Resources must be committed on a global scale to work out global problems.

[The Peaceful Use of Resources]

A powerful means of achieving this is to maintain and promote a peaceful international environment and strive for arms reduction. The redundant power arising from such attempts should be shifted to the settlement of global problems. In recent years, the world's military expenditure has risen continuously. Developing nations, in particular, have been increasing their share of military spending. Also of late there have been moves among developed countries to expand armaments.

However, there is a certain aspect in which the longer a peaceful period prevails the more difficult it is to preserve peace. This is because the number of people who have experienced the horrors and disturbance of war are decreasing. In Japan, the ratio of those born in postwar years — the generation which does not know war — to the entire population is expected to rise from 54% in 1980 to 72% in the year 2000. In such a situation it is necessary for all those concerned to make more efforts than before to preserve and further promote a peaceful environment.

b.  Accommodating the North-South Problem

The North-South problem is one of the most serious questions confronting mankind at present.

Throughout the past 20 years, the North-South gap has remained wide. At present, developing countries (including China) account for 3/4 of the world's population. However, their total income share is merely 1/5 of the world total and their per-capita income is less than 1/10th that of industrially advanced nations.

Also, many people in developing nations, centering around the least developed countries, are suffering from malnutrition. According to FAO, there were about 490 million people suffering from malnutrition in 1980, whose nutritious intake was less than the minimum required amount.

Under these circumstances, there has been a conspicuous trend towards divergence — the so-called South-South problem — among the developing countries. Non-oil producing developing countries are confronted with large deficits in their current accounts and an accumulation of external debts.

[Prospects for the North-South Problem]

As seen in Chapter 2, the developing countries are expected to accomplish higher economic growth than industrially developed nations on the average in future. However, a large gap is likely to continue between the North and South in per-capita income.

Also, divergence in economic performance will go ahead in future, with the middle income developing nations likely to continue a favorable economic performance. However, low income developing countries, particularly in south Asia and the least developed zones in Africa south of the Sahara, will remain sluggish. The question of malnutrition is also expected to become more serious.

The future trend for the energy situation will largely affect the economic growth of non-oil producing developing nations. Deficits in the international balance of payments will continue to be a strong primary restrictive factor.

[Development Strategy for Developing Nations]

The question of how to make progress in industrialization will be an important issue for developing nations in their paths towards autonomous economic development. It is important for them to obtain proper technology, develop good personnel and promote small businesses. It is also important for them to develop agriculture, not only for a steady maintenance of foodstuffs, but also for securing smooth industrialization.

Also, in considering a future development strategy and economic cooperation to support it, it will be necessary for Japan to respond to each nation's stage of development on the basis of that nation's inherent historical and social conditions.

[Economic Cooperation for the 21st Century]

Economic cooperation is a very important field in which Japan, a nation in possession of great economic power and in close contact with developing countries, can contribute to the development of a world economic society, and furthermore, to world peace. Therefore, Japan must drastically expand its private economic cooperation and official development assistance on the way to the 21st century, cooperate with other industrially advanced nations and take the lead in actively dealing with the settlement of the North-South issue.

The following are what Japan can do towards such a goal:

First, with respect to private economic cooperation, Japan has had close economic relations with developing nations in trade and direct investment. Japan should offer its powerful export market and promote transfers of capital and management know-how by positively opening up its market and implementing smooth industrial coordination and direct private investment. Japan should also transfer the proper technology suitable for the development phase.

Second, it is necessary for the government to promote both positive and efficient official development assistance. For the moment, the government should try to steadily accomplish the mid-term goal of its official development assistance plan formulated in January 1981. Looking into the 21st century, the government should also systematically push ahead with its official long-term development assistance, and make efforts to raise the amount of such assistance to the level befitting Japan's international position.

Third, Japan should make positive use of as many talented Japanese human resources as possible in the international cooperative arena supporting the developing nations. It should also promote cooperation in the training of technical experts and skilled workers as well as the building up of human resources in developing countries.

c. Accommodation of Various Problems on a Global Scale

[Accommodation of Environmental Problems on a Global Scale]

As witnessed in Chapter 2, the tackling of environmental problems on a global scale, such as rises in the density of carbon dioxide, desertification and ecological destruction will become more important issues than ever before.

It is necessary for all concerned to take full note of preserving the natural environment around us from a long-term viewpoint, because once it is changed, it will take enormous time and money to bring it back to its original form.

Also, international cooperation is indispensable because these environmental changes take place beyond national boundaries. It is necessary to pay full attention to maintaining compatibility between economic growth and preserving the environment, especially in international cooperation with the developing countries lacking in both the technology to preserve the environment and economic power.

[Projects on a Global Scale]

It is necessary to press forward with a large-scale global project involving all nations, in order to deal with the problems of foodstuffs and the environment on a global scale and further the development of developing countries.

In future, it will be possible for Japan to make global contributions in making use of its technology, capital and human resources, previously employed for domestic development, in undertakings on a global scale.

## Section 2 The Aging Society and Comfortable Living Conditions

From now until the 21st century, Japanese economic society will face a number of difficult issues, particularly the trend towards an aging population. In this section, we will look into a basic strategy for creating an aging society with comfortable living conditions for the people as a whole, which also accommodates various economic and social problems arising thereof.

[Thinking on the Aging Trend]

Japan will undoubtedly move on to become an aging society in future. A society with people of advanced age that will exist in the 21st century will be a new experience for us. We must cope with many problems in the meantime. In considering these problems, we must take note of the following:

First of all, it is not correct to merely accept the idea of an aging society itself half-heartedly. The fact that there are many aged people means that Japan is a nation with a long life-span in one aspect and that there are many people rich in knowledge and experience. We should not look at an aging society in negative terms. It is important for each of us to develop the understanding and right frame of mind for an aging society at an early stage, and try to enrich our thoughts on it.

Second, it is necessary for us not to be excessively pessimistic about problems when we run into unknown variations. The shift towards an aging society in future will force both social and economic fields, and others, to come up with various accommodations. However, we have so far conquered the changes in various domestic and external conditions. It is fully possible for us to carry out a smooth transfer if we grasp the problems correctly and make appropriate responses, given the long-term trend we are now facing.

## 1. Various Problems in the Trend Towards Aging

(1) The Trend Towards an Aging Labor Force and Securing a Balance Between Demand and Supply of Labor

In connection with the trend towards an aging population, the tendency towards an aging labor force will make rapid progress in future. Furthermore, there will be special characteristics such as a rapid rise in the tempo of aging, and a high ratio of the labor force composed of older people in Japan compared with the United States and advanced Western nations. Thus, the tendency towards an aging labor force will move ahead at a quicker tempo in Japan than other countries.

[Ratio of Labor Force in Old Age Group]
    In looking at a comparison of the ratio of the labor force in old age groups (55 or older) between Japan and the United States and advanced Western nations, there are the following special features (See Table 3-2-1): (1) the ratio is higher in Japan than the U.S. and European countries both for men and women, and (2) Japan is far ahead of the U.S. and European nations, particularly in the number of those who are 65 or older.
    The ratio of the labor force consisting of those who are 65 or older in Japan has, in recent years, been in decline due to increases in income along with the growth in the country's economy, and a reduction in the number of people engaging in agricultural and forestry work. However, due to the effect of various primary factors including the people's sense of value for work and the formation of families, it is believed that Japan is maintaining a higher ratio than the U.S. and European nations.

— 118 —

**Table 3-2-1 An International Comparison of Aged Labor Forces**

(In %)

| | U.S. (1981) | Canada (1980) | West Germany (1980) | France (March 1981) | Japan (1980) |
|---|---|---|---|---|---|
| Men | | | | | |
| 55—64 years old | 70.8 | 76.5 | 71.4 | 64.3 | 88.7 |
| 65 or older | 18.5 | 14.9 | 7.8 | 7.3 | 45.4 |
| Women | | | | | |
| 55—64 years old | 41.5 | 33.8 | 29.1 | 37.6 | 45.5 |
| 65 or older | 8.1 | 4.1 | 3.0 | 2.9 | 15.6 |

**Sources:**
(U.S.) Department of Labor "Employment and Earnings";
(Canada) Statistics Canada "The labour force, October 1980";
(West Germany) Bundesministerium für Arbeit und
Sozialordnung "Arbeits und Sozialstatistik"; (France) Institut
National de la Statistique et des Etudes Economiques
"Enquete Sur L'emplor"; (Japan) Statistics Bureau of the
Prime Minister's Office "Census."

It is assumed that the decline in the ratio of the aged in the labor
force will continue in Japan in future, but because it is considered that
there will be no major change in the people's sense of value for work,
Japan will retain a higher ratio than the U.S. and European countries.

[Progress in the Trend Towards an Aging Labor Force]
Taking the ratio of manpower into consideration as a precondition,
the tendency towards an aging labor force is expected to move forward
rapidly along with the overall trend towards an aging society. Now, in
considering people of advanced age by dividing them into one group
with those "under 65 and older than 54" and another with those "65
and above," it is expected that between 1980 and the year 2000: (1)
those below 65 and older than 54 (between 55 and 64 years old) will
increase by 6.10 million and their share in Japan's population aged 15
or older will rise from 11.3% to 15.3%, and (2) those 65 or older will

**Table 3-2-2   Trend Toward Advanced Age in Labor Population**

(In thousand people, %)

|  | 1980 | 2000 | Increase |
|---|---|---|---|
| (Population) | | | |
| Those under 65 years old | 10,097 ( 11.3) | 16,200 ( 15.3) | 6,103 |
| Those 65 years old or older | 10,574 ( 11.8) | 19,942 ( 18.9) | 9,368 |
| Total of those 15 years old or older | 89,330 (100.0) | 105,555 (100.0) | 16,225 |
| (Labor population) | | | |
| Those under 65 years old | 6,521 ( 11.4) | 11,052 ( 16.9) | 4,531 |
| Those 65 years old or older | 2,986 ( 5.2) | 4,645 ( 7.1) | 1,659 |
| Total of those 15 years old or older | 57,069 (100.0) | 65,297 (100.0) | 8,228 |

**Notes:**

1. **Sources:** Statistics Bureau of the Prime Minister's Office "Census"; Institute of Population Problems of the Ministry of Health and Welfare "Future Population Projections for Japan by Sex-Age for 1980-2080 (November 1981). The Figures are based on medium variant and estimated by the Planning Bureau of the Economic Planning Agency.
2. Those under 65 years old include those aged 55 to 64.
3. Figures in the parentheses represent ratios of composition.

increase by 9.37 million and their share will go up from 11.8% to 18.9% (See Table 3-2-2).

Looking at this in terms of labor population, those "under 65 and older than 54" will rise by 4.53 million, increasing from 11.4% to 16.9% in their share of the labor force, and those who are "65 or older" will increase by 1.66 million, raising their share from 5.2% to 7.1%. (The reason why there is not much noticeable increase in the number of those "65 or older" in the labor population compared with the total population of the country, is because their ratio in the work force is considerably lower than that of those "under 65 and older than 54 years old.")

Looking at these people in the 1980s and 1990s, it is expected that those "under 65" will rise conspicuously in the 1980s, while those

"65 or older" will increase in the same range as those "under 65" in the 1990s. As a result, those especially "under 65" will show a large increase by the year 2000, with the amount of increase totaling 4.53 million and accounting for 55% of 8.23 million, the estimated total increase in the labor force during the same period.

Furthermore, after the year 2000, the so-called postwar baby boom generation will find itself in the advanced age group (55 or older). Thus, the aging trend will further accelerate at a rapid tempo.


[The Trend Towards an Aging Labor Force and the Supply and Demand of Labor]

The tendency towards an aging labor force mentioned above will bring about a major change in the supply and demand relations of labor, requiring diversified coordination.

It is difficult to accurately look into variations in the age composition of the labor force for different industries over the next 20 years. Therefore, some trial figures are offered here to determine what degree of gap there will be in the supply and demand of labor according to age, in case the trend in recent years of an employment pattern according to age for different industries continues in future (See Table 3-2-3).

According to these trial figures, there will be a considerable excess of demand for those in the 15-29 age group in industry as a whole. Conversely, there will be an excess supply of those aged 30 or older. By industry, industry in upstream areas will feature increased demand for a labor force of relatively advanced age, while increases in the number of those aged 15-29 will result in industry in downstream areas.

Of course, this gap appearing in the supply and demand of labor is the result of a simple comparison between the supply and demand for labor expected in the event that the demand for labor according to age in each industry in recent years continues within the framework of the present wage system and employment practice. No attempt was made to forecast any such actual gap. However, it is presumed that there will be a large gap in supply and demand if the present situation remains the same. It is feared that there will be a mismatch of supply and demand for those belonging to the age group under 65, particularly when they fail to cope with smooth changes in the supply and demand for labor. We are afraid, therefore, that there will be strong pressure on

**Table 3-2-3　The Prospect for Supply and Demand of Male Labor According to Group**

| | Demand for labor force | | | | Supply in labor force |
|---|---|---|---|---|---|
| Ratio of composition according to age group (%) | Agriculture, forestry and fisheries industry | Upstream industry | Downstream industry | Total in industry | |
| (1980) | | | | | |
| 15 — 29 years old | 9.1 | 23.4 | 25.1 | 23.0 | 23.2 |
| 30 — 54 years old | 46.8 | 64.0 | 60.5 | 60.6 | 60.0 |
| 55 — 64 years old | 23.9 | 9.3 | 9.7 | 10.8 | 11.1 |
| 65 or older | 20.1 | 3.2 | 4.8 | 5.6 | 5.7 |
| (2000) | | | | | |
| 15 — 29 years old | 5.3 | 22.4 | 36.8 | 30.4 | 22.2 |
| 30 — 54 years old | 29.7 | 51.7 | 45.9 | 47.0 | 53.0 |
| 55 — 64 years old | 23.6 | 20.0 | 12.0 | 15.4 | 16.9 |
| 65 or older | 41.3 | 6.0 | 5.2 | 7.0 | 7.9 |
| Multiplying ratio (2000/1980) | | | | | |
| 15 — 29 years old | 0.380 | 1.009 | 1.994 | 1.554 | 1.099 |
| 30 — 54 years old | 0.416 | 0.853 | 1.027 | 0.911 | 1.014 |
| 55 — 64 years old | 0.648 | 2.263 | 1.684 | 1.666 | 1.745 |
| 65 or older | 1.348 | 1.990 | 1.453 | 1.536 | 1.595 |

**Sources:**

Statistics Bureau of the Prime Minister's Office "Census"; estimates by the Planning Bureau of the Economic Planning Agency.

the labor market to adjust. Thus, policy accommodations will be in demand, and voices calling for changes in the existing wage system and employment practices are expected to become louder.

[Demand for Labor under Medium Growth]
As we take a view of the prospective supply and demand for labor going into the year 2000, we will have to face the following environmental changes in addition to the question of aging.

First, labor supply and demand must be coordinated under the medium growth of the nation's economy.

In future the growth in absolute demand for labor under the medium growth of the economy will not be so extensive. According to the results of the study made on model cases in long-term multiple sectors in Chapter 2, the balance in labor supply and demand could be preserved, on the whole, if the trend towards the reduction of actual working hours can be continued under the condition of about 4% growth. However, it may become necessary for those concerned to make efforts to carry out smooth occupational changes in order to meet variations in the industrial structure amidst the sluggish growth in total demand.

[Appearance of Women in the Labor Market]
Second, there is the matter of women making their presence felt in the labor market. It is anticipated that the movement of women in the labor market will show considerable differences according to age group in future (See Table 3-2-4).

It is expected that the female labor force in the 15-29 age group will tend to decline because the growth rate in the population of this particular group is low, the ratio of people in this category seeking higher education will increase, and, if the birth rate recovers as reported in terms of a medium variant by the Institute of Population Problems of the Health and Welfare Ministry, some mothers will have to devote themselves to child rearing. However, growth in the ratio of labor force for women older than this category is anticipated. In particular, large growth is expected in the group for women aged between 55 and 64, so it is anticipated that the labor force will also register large growth.

Consequently, the total female labor force will increase from

**Table 3-2-4　The Outlook for the Female Work Force According to Age Group**

(In thousand people, %)

|  | 1970 | 1980 | 1990 | 2000 |
|---|---|---|---|---|
| 15—29 years old | 7,439 ( 36.1) | 5,729 ( 26.7) | 5,771 ( 24.1) | 5,374 ( 22.0) |
| 30—54 years old | 10,260 ( 49.7) | 12,238 ( 57.0) | 13,534 ( 56.5) | 13,501 ( 55.3) |
| 55—64 years old | 2,123 ( 10.3) | 2,561 ( 11.9) | 3,587 ( 15.0) | 4,142 ( 17.0) |
| 65 or older | 808 ( 3.9) | 959 ( 4.5) | 1,053 ( 4.4) | 1,414 ( 5.8) |
| Total of those who are 15 years old or older | 20,630 (100.0) | 21,487 (100.0) | 23,946 (100.0) | 24,430 (100.0) |

**Notes:**

1. **Sources:** Statistics Bureau of the Prime Minister's Office "Census" and estimates by the Planning Bureau of the Economic Planning Agency.

2. Figures in parentheses represent ratios of composition.

21,490,000 in 1980 to 24,430,000 in the year 2000, but its proportion of the total labor force will level off from 37.7% to 37.4%.

[The Trend Towards Higher Education in the Labor Force]

Third, there is a trend among Japanese workers to seek higher education.

The percentage of Japanese people wishing to receive higher education has been rising rapidly since the 1960s. This rising tempo itself is likely to slow down in future, but reflecting the increase in percentage of those who received higher education in the past, the proportion of people with higher education among those in advanced age groups is expected to increase in future. And, on the whole, the trend towards higher education for labor is likely to progress (See Table 3-2-5).

[Effects of the Spread of Technical Innovation]

Fourth, there is the effect of technical innovation, particularly that of micro electronics (ME).

Technical innovation, which has made rapid progress of late in micro electronics, has propagated industrial robots and office automation (OA). It is expected to spread over wide-ranging areas,

**Table 3-2-5    The Percentage of People with Higher Education among Those Aged 20 or Older in the Population**

(In %)

|        | 1970 | 1980 | 1990 | 2000 |
|--------|------|------|------|------|
| Men    | 16.6 | 20.8 | 25.5 | 29.7 |
| Women  | 6.4  | 11.3 | 15.8 | 20.0 |
| Total  | 11.5 | 15.9 | 20.5 | 24.7 |

**Notes:**
1. **Sources:** Statistics Bureau of the Prime Minister's Office "Census"; Ministry of Education "Fundamental Study of Schools"; estimates by the Planning Bureau of the Economic Planning Agency.
2. "People with higher education" refers to those who are graduates or students of universities, colleges and special professional schools.
3. The rate of people's advance into higher education in 1982 and beyond is based on an estimate worked out against the 1981 percentage used as a fixed number.

engulfing big enterprises as well as medium- and small-sized companies, and production sites as well as office management, sales, special and technical occupation fields.

With respect to the effects of technical innovation on employment, there are both pessimistic and optimistic views. The former believes there will be progress in labor saving, a decline in the demand for labor, and a loss of opportunities for employment. The latter believes there will be increased demand for labor in new services, new kinds of jobs and industries which will generate new jobs, and that therefore, there will be no decline in demand for labor on the whole. Up till now, the predominant view has been confident about employment. However, it will be necessary for us to keep a careful watch on the situation in future because the progress in technical innovation is likely to bring about diversified effects in the employment situation as time passes.

## (2) Social Security in the Aging Society

Social security is an important pillar designed to sustain the people's lifestyles and social stability, by completing the fundamental conditions necessary for people to maintain their life plans without fear at any stage of their lives. Its role is expected to become more important, especially concerning both the guarantee of income and maintenance of health for old people, as wel go into the 21st century amidst the current aging trend. However, because the present social security program is not made to fully accommodate the future aging society, it should be reformed to meet the needs of the future aging society.

### a. The Present Social Security System and Its Future

[The Present Social Security System]
As we look back at social security in Japan, we know that efforts have been made in various fields to make it more substantial, particularly in the latter half of the 1960s against the background of economic growth. As a result, the social security system in our country can stand comparison with the United States and European countries.

However, Japan is not on a par with America and European nations in the scale of the social security program available at present as seen in Figure 3-2-6. (This is the proportion of social security payments in national income). This is because Japan has not yet witnessed the progress of the aging society as much as America and Europe with the subsequent pension system. It is anticipated that the scale of the Japanese social security system will be expanded as the society ages and the pension system meets ever-increasing needs.

[The Future for Pensions]
Within the aging process of society towards the 21st century, let us consider what sort of shape the scale of social security will take, by dividing it into pensions and medical payments.

It is anticipated that pension payments and the cost of this burden will increase rapidly concomitant with the aging society and maturity of the pension system.

The degree of maturity of the public pension system in Japan is

## Fig. 3-2-6   The Scope of the Social Security System and Its International Comparison

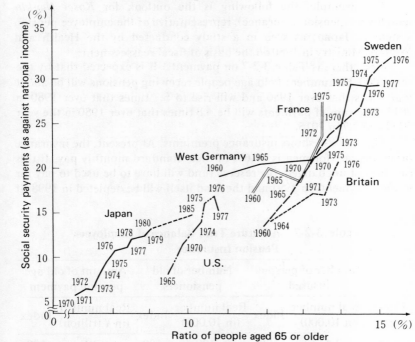

**Notes:**

1. **Sources:** ILO "The Cost of Social Security," U.N. "Demographic Yearbook," OECD "National Accounts of OECD Countries" and Ministry of Health and Welfare "Cost of Social Security Payment."
2. The cost of social security payments refers to benefits in "the cost of social security" in ILO reference material.
3. As for 1980 and 1985 in Japan, the numerical value is the ratio of social security transfers against national income. The numerical value for 1985 is a hypothesis made in Japan's new 7-year economic and social program.
4. Social security payments in the U.S. and Britain take place in the fiscal year and their national income is calculated for the calendar year.

still low on the whole, and it will take another 30 years before it reaches maturity.

For example, the following is the outlook for *Kosei Nenkin* (employees' pension insurance), representative of the employee pension system in Japan, as seen in a study conducted by the Health and Welfare Ministry in 1980 on the basis of fiscal reassessment.

First, there is Table 3-2-7 on payments. It is expected that by the year 2000 the number of old age people receiving pensions will be about four times that over 1980 and will rise to 5.7 times that over 1980 in 2015. The sum of payments will be 4.8 times that over 1980 in the year 2000 and 7.7 in 2015.

Figure 3-2-8 shows insurance premiums. At present, the insurance premium rate for men is 10.6% of their standard monthly pay. If this rate is kept unchanged, the reserve fund will have to be used to pay for welfare payments in 1991 and the fund itself will be depleted in 1998. If

**Table 3-2-7    A Future Trial Balance of Employees' Pension Insurance**

| Fiscal year | Number of persons insured | | Number of old pensioners | | Amount of old age pension payment | |
|---|---|---|---|---|---|---|
| | Real number (in 10,000) | Index | Real number (in 10,000) | Index | Real number (in ¥ trillion) | Index |
| 1980 | 2,472 | 100 | 199 | 100 | 2.1 | 100 |
| 1990 | 2,768 | 112 | 461 | 232 | 5.5 | 263 |
| 2000 | 3,033 | 123 | 767 | 385 | 10.0 | 481 |
| 2010 | 3,105 | 126 | 1,046 | 525 | 14.6 | 704 |
| 2015 | 3,103 | 126 | 1,136 | 570 | 16.2 | 771 |
| 2020 | 3,162 | 128 | 1,168 | 587 | 16.7 | 795 |

**Notes:**
1. **Source:** Pension Bureau of the Health and Welfare Ministry "Results of Financial Recalculations of Employees' Pension Insurance and National Pensions in 1980."
2. The amount of pension payment is in terms of fiscal 1980 prices.
3. The numerical value is the index worked out against 100 in fiscal 1980.

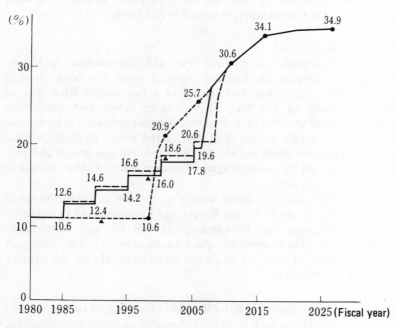

Notes:
1. **Source:** Same as Table 3-2-7.
2.  —— in case a 1.8% increase is realized every five years.
    ---- in case a 2.0% increase is realized every five years.
    ------ in case 10.6% is left untouched.
3.  ▲ the fiscal year when the revenue-expenditure fund becomes
    negative.

the present level of payment is still retained after 1998, the pension
system will have to be shifted to a levy system under which the annual
pension payment must be supported by the annual premium income
provided by employees. The insurance premium rate will reach 21% in
the year 2000 and about 34% in 2015, the year in which it will reach
maturity. Otherwise, there will be no balance between revenue and ex-

penditure. Incidentally, according to the Institute of Population Problems of the Health and Welfare Ministry in its "Future Population Projections for Japan by Sex-Age for 1980-2080" (medium variant) in November 1981, this ratio is expected to rise further.

[Future Medical Costs]
It is anticipated that medical costs will also increase in future. The rate of increase in national medical costs has been slowing down recently, but it has been rising at a rate higher than that of national income in the face of the aging trend and qualitative improvements in medical care. In particular, old age medical costs have been rising at a rate higher than that of the entire medical cost for implementing free medical care for the aged. By age group, the per-head medical cost for patients aged 70 or over is four to five times that over the 30-34 age group.

As the tempo of the aging society accelerates in future, medical costs centering on medical care for the aged are expected to continue increasing. Against this background, it will become increasingly important for Japan to consider which medical costs it will cover and the effectiveness of such an emphasis while maintaining the present level of medical service.

[Social Security Transfers and the Prospects for Burdens on the System]
Let us now take a look at a trial balance of social security transfers and the burden, on the whole, on the social security insurance system, given the situation mentioned above.

Future social security transfers and their burden will move in a direction as shown in Table 3-2-9 in the event the present system is retained on the premise of the population picture described in Chapter 2.

First, the proportion of social security transfers in national income is expected to rise from 12.8% in fiscal 1980 to about 23% in the year 2000 and 37% in 2025. In particular, pension payments will accelerate their rapid rise from 4.3% in fiscal 1980 to about 12% in the year 2000 and about 19% in 2025.

In connection with this, the cost of social security and ordinary transfers from the central and local governments will increase rapidly. In other words, the pension burden will climb from 4.9% in fiscal 1980

**Table 3-2-9    The Transfers and Burden of the Social Security
Insurance System**

(In %)

| Fiscal year | | 1980 | 2000 | 2025 |
|---|---|---|---|---|
| 1. | Total social security payments | 10.1 | Around 20 | Around 32 |
| | (1)  Pension | 4.3 | "  12 | "  19 |
| | (2)  Medical cost | 4.9 | "  7 | "  12 |
| | (3)  Others | 0.9 | "  1 | "  1 |
| 2. | Social assistance fund | 2.8 | "  3 | "  5 |
| 3. | Social transfer (= 1 + 2) | 12.8 | "  23 | "  37 |
| 4. | Total social security burden | 9.3 | Around 15 | Around 24 |
| | (1)  Pension | 4.9 | "  9 | "  16 |
| | (2)  Medical cost | 3.5 | "  5 | "  7 |
| | (3)  Others | 0.9 | "  1 | "  1 |
| 5. | Ordinary transfers from central and local governments | 3.0 | "  5 | "  9 |

**Notes:**
1. **Sources:** Economic Planning Agency "Annual Report on
   National Accounts" and estimates by the Planning Bureau of
   the Economic Planning Agency.
2. The numerical value is the ratio against national income.
3. The numerical value is that of when the present system is
   preserved.

to about 9% in the year 2000 and about 16% in 2025. Ordinary
transfers from both central and local governments will increase from
3.0% in fiscal 1980 to about 5% in the year 2000 and about 9% in 2025,
along with rapid rises in pension and medical payments.

Within this process, social security fund deposits (the increase in
pension reserves), now at about the 3% level of national income, will
decline gradually, dropping to a minus (breakdown of the reserve fund)
in the 1990s and plunging to zero in fiscal 2000.

If, hypothetically, a change was made in the *Kosei Nenkin* system,
such as raising the age of those eligible to receive a pension, or revising
the standard for pension payments, its effect on a trial balance would
be as follows:

(1)   If the age of those eligible to receive pensions was raised by five years, the rate of insurance premiums in fiscal 2025 would decline about 5 percentage points. (If the system remained unchanged, according to a trial balance worked out in November 1981 by the Institute of Population Problems of the Health and Welfare Ministry in terms of a medium variant based on the population of the country, the current 10.6% insurance premium rate for men would rise to about 40% in fiscal 2025. But if the age of those eligible to receive pensions was raised by five years, the percentage would be like the one mentioned above.)

(2)   If the standard for pension payments, as anticipated in fiscal 2025 under the present system, was dropped by 10% on average among those eligible to receive it, the rate of insurance premium would decline by about 4 percentage points. (If the system remained unaltered, the ratio of the sum of old age pension payments as against the standard monthly salary would be increased from 49% in fiscal 1980 to about 65% in fiscal 2025, on average, among those eligible to receive it, because of the trend towards a longer average period of participation in the pension program. But if restraint was put on the payment standard, the rate of insurance premium would come down as stated above.)

b.   Changes in the Burden Between Generations

If the social security transfer and its burden move about in this way in future and occupy a major portion of the national economy, the most serious problem will be a destruction of the balance between those receiving the benefits and those sharing the burden between generations. And, there will also be the fear of losing economic and social vitality.

[The Balance Between Present and Future Generations]
Changes in the burden between generations will first be the relations between present and future generations. Let us now set up a standard wage earners' income pattern for *Kosei Nenkin* pensions (starting basic monthly pay 100,000 yen, monthly wage at the time of retirement 300,000 yen, average monthly pay 200,000 yen for a person aged 40 with 35 years of employment and his wife also aged 40), assume that the yield on the reserve fund's operation, wages and consumer price

deflator are all at the same rate and consider each amount of money in terms of fiscal 1980 prices. Considering this on the premise of the present average remainder of the Japanese people (35.5 years for men and 40.3 years for women), those who are eligible to receive pensions under the present system will get a total sum of 33,860,000 yen per person. On the other hand, each person earns a total of 84,000,000 yen in monthly salary during the period of their employment. Under the present system, 20% of the pension payment is supposed to be covered by the nation, and the amount of payment to be furnished in insuranced premiums paid by salaried men and women should be 32.2% of their total monthly earnings (33,860,000 yen × 0.8 ÷ 84,000,000 yen). The insurance premium rate under the existing system is 10.6%, about 1/3 of what it is supposed to be.

Consequently, if the present situation continues, about 6.4 trillion yen will be collected as insurance premiums every year, yet, on the other hand, there will be a gap of 15.7 trillion yen since pension payments are expected to total 22.1 trillion yen in future. Similarly, there will be a gap of 6.0 trillion yen in *Kokumin Nenkin* (national pensions) and 4.5 trillion yen in *Kyosai Nenkin* (mutual benefit pensions).

Since the present system should not be left untouched, a shift to an imposition system may become necessary as the pension system attains maturity.

At any rate, future generations must shoulder this monetary burden in some manner; therefore under the present system, current generations are leaving a very large burden for future generations to cope with.

[The Balance Between the Working and Aging Generations]
The second issue in the so-called "burden between generations" is the change in relations between the working and aging generations.

In taking into consideration the example of the aforementioned *Kosei Nenkin* (employees' pension insurance), the working generation must pay 32.2% of their monthly wage for insurance per head (16.1% to be deducted from the monthly salary since enterprises pay half) at the time when the pension system reaches maturity. The average monthly take home pay per person after the insurance premium is deducted will be 168,000 yen. Each old age household (those who are eligible to receive a pension) will obtain 157,000 yen. However, the working household may have extra income, such as bonuses, while the aging household may have the wife's *Kokumin Nenkin* (national pension).

It is rather difficult to come up with a model calculation taking into account all these points mentioned above. Working households will probably have more family members and thus be faced with their children's educational expenses, supporting them and saving some necessary money in preparation for old age. In taking these into consideration, it is possible to believe that the present pension system is designed to keep the income of the aging household at a high standard compared with the working household.

[Effects on the Vitality of the Economic Society]

The above-mentioned change in relations between those who receive the benefit and those who must shoulder the burden between generations may lead to a necessary re-study of the system from the standpoint of fairness. Furthermore, such a change may spoil the vitality of the economic society.

For one thing, there will be an effect on the change in rate of deposits. The high standard to be provided by the official annuity system will lead to a decline in the need for the people to save money in preparation for their old age, and may move in a direction toward reducing the rate of family savings.

Also, under a social security system lacking in balance, there is a possibility that workers will lose the desire to work because of their heavy tax burden and social security insurance and this imbalance may cause a decline in incentives for enterprise and individual management activities.

From the standpoint of these possibilities, the choices for the system implemented at present concerning social security will not only change regarding income transfers just in the period presently under review, but will also leave the burden for future generations to shoulder and damage the vitality of the economy in its entirety.

It is our major responsibility to complete a proper, balanced social security plan between generations and establish a viable economic social framework for future generations to inherit.

(3)  Other Important Problems

In addition to the problems mentioned above, it is believed that the following issues will confront our society in future.

[The Need for Welfare and Keeping the Aged Healthy]
In connection with the shift towards an aging society, keeping the aged in good health will become an important issue.

Whether or not the aged are healthy in mind and body will affect the substance of their lives. This will considerably depend on such factors as the way they lived before old age. Therefore, their efforts to maintain daily health will have significant meaning. Thus, it is important for us to support them positively in such measures as to maintain individual efforts to sustain health.

On the other hand, it is inevitable for people becoming old to be in need of assistance and for us to witness increases in their number suffering from illness. It is expected that medical and welfare needs will rise. In particular, in considering the number of so-called aged people lying in bed in relation to the population ratio according to age groups in a certain fixed calculation, it is anticipated that the number of such people will rise by about double in the year 2000 compared with about 510,000 people in 1981. The mental, physical and economic burden shared by families with aged members in bed will be heavy. So it is expected that there will be a call for the expansion of welfare measures for such families.

[Consideration for the Handicapped]
There has been a rising trend towards increases in the number of the physically handicapped, with the ratio in the nation's population jumping from 1.8% in 1970 to 2.4% in 1980.

The number of physically handicapped will rise by more than 50% in the year 2000 and there will an aging tendency among them, if we assume that the ratio in the population according to age groups proceeds at the present rate.

In the midst of it, there will be a request for further substantial measures to assist the physically handicapped in the fields of health and medical care, welfare service, employment, work and education.

As stated above, in our society in future, more consideration for the physically handicapped will be requested.

[The Healthy Rearing of Younger Generations]
In the wake of a decline in the number of children, increases in material affluence and convenience, a reduction of opportunities to be in touch with nature, and the intensity of school entrance examination competition, problems have arisen concerning the shortage of places and chances for young people to undergo sound mental and physical training, increases in the number of parents either providing excessive protection for their children or leaving them alone, and a downward tendency among the people in the sense of their relationship with society.

In order to make the coming aging society rich in vitality and broad-minded, the healthy rearing of young people who will support the future aging society will become an extremely important issue. Proper accommodations in wide ranging fields including the home, school and social education to the realization of young people equipped with independent spirit, care for mutual relations, and social affability will be in demand.

(4)   The Need to Design a Japanese-Style Aging Society

In order to resolve many issues such as the trend towards an aging labor force as mentioned above, and social security, it is necessary for us to both consult the experience of Western welfare society as well as make use of Japan's own characteristic social conditions and draw up designs for a creative Japanese-type aging society by placing the roles of employment, pensions, saving deposits and the home in proper perspective, rather than responding to individual issues separately.

[The Existing Japanese-Type System]
It is said that the era of high economic growth in Japanese society began in the face of a rising young population sustained by a high birth rate, and that the employment pattern was shaped with a continued rise in productive age population as a given condition (seniority system, etc.) as well as families, employment and assets being formed with the rearing of those aged zero to 15 chiefly in mind.

— 136 —

Looking at this from the overall point of view of stage of life and income transfers from generation to generation, it has been the normal pattern in Japan that parents assumed the responsibility of supporting their children until they finished their school education. They have also gained support in old age from their children in the prime of their earning lives.

[Population Movement Forcing Change in the Existing System; Changes in Life Span]

However, population movement and changes in life span in recent years have tended to force alterations in the existing system.

First, the productive age population will peak in 1995 at 86,900,000 from 78,970,000 in 1980, and the tempo of decline will accelerate gradually to 85,620,000 in the year 2000 and to 78,750,000 in 2020.

Second, as a result of the decline in birth rate and extension of life span, the composition of the dependent population centering on those aged 0 to 15 will change to that of people aged 65 or over. Looking at this in terms of the aging society index (the number of those aged 65 or over/those aged 0 to 15), the percentage will move from 19% in 1960 to 38% in 1980, 88% in the year 2000 and 130% in 2020.

Third, the average life span will undergo a major change as a result of the extension of one's life time and a reduction of working hours.

When the average life span used to be 50 years in Japan. The life span in the country was such that the parents' life expectancy came to an end when their offspring grew from childhood to adolescence. And little importance was paid to the Japanese people in the period of their old age. Now, the present life span of people in this country has been extended to 80 years. In this new era, it means that even after children reach adolescence, their parents still have 1/3 of their life span remaining. Most important of all is how they spend this period of their life.

[The Need for an Aged Society to Live Comfortably]

The need to establish regions and communities for the aged to live in comfortably will a rise in society as a whole, as it becomes important for each person to consider how he or she should live in old age while the nation simultaneously shifts towards an aging society.

The people who will retire from their active careers and join in the formation of the aged group towards the 21st century will be those who have lived in turbulent periods, supported the era of high economic growth in Japan and helped establish the country's present economic affluence. It is the duty of the succeeding generation to assist these people in building an affluent society in which they can live well.

[Diversified Range of Choice]

In drawing up designs for a Japanese style aging society in future, we need not necessarily be confronted with limited and narrow paths but rather have diversified choices to tread creative paths.

First, with respect to work, the aged in our country have a relatively high degree of desire to work compared with old aged people in Europe and America. Therefore, it is highly possible to sketch a design of an aging society directed at paying respect to the aged for their working ability and desire.

Second, there is still considerable time left for Japan before social security comes to full maturity. Also, the situation on problems which will emerge in future is relatively clear. On the other hand, the Japanese people's saving habits do not incorporate the idea of a social security system in its maturity. They have not lessened their desire to save for old age. Thus, it is still possible for us to appreciate properly the various future effects on many different areas and establish a social security system suitable for the aging society.

Third, there have been some changes in recent years in the family in Japan. However, considering the Japanese people's thinking on living together with parents or on divorce, the Japanese sense of value of the home is fundamentally closer to that of Asia than Europe and America. And, it is possible to expect the home to positively function as fundamental to supporting society with its vital force, provided that its role in society is properly positioned and that efforts are made to substantiate its basic foundation.

Under the aforementioned perception, it is necessary for us to deepen dialogue in various fields in future on the ideal way of setting up a Japanese style aging society.

## 2. A Basic Strategy for an Aging Society Comfortable to Live In

Japan must settle a number of major issues given the aging trend mentioned previously, and construct a society in which its people can live comfortably.

What is important in this case is that not only the aged, but all other people making up the society must be able to live an enriched life. For this purpose, it is necessary for us to pursue a society based on the following four doctrines as we move on to the 21st century.

[Four Doctrines for the 21st Century]

The First is the establishment of a "society in which individuals can demonstrate their ability freely and which can respond to diversified needs." It must be a highly flexible society in accommodating the diversification of sense of value, the aging of the population, and women's activities in society. It should be a society in which responsible individuals can freely display their competency regardless of age, sex and the presence of obstacles, and a society which can answer to individuals' diversified needs.

The second is a "balanced and fair society." The projected society must be balanced and fair in striking a pertinent balance between those receiving benefits and those sharing the burden in various social strata, based on various social systems and customs.

The third is a "tolerant society." It must be a society in which the aged and the handicapped can live their lives either at home, their place of work or in the community and can participate in social activities while children are brought up in good health.

The fourth is a "society which can accommodate the progress in internationalization." It is necessary to establish a society in which the people in every stratum correctly deepen their understanding of internationalization, while each nucleus can fully perceive its role and responsibility in international society, and conduct activities accordingly.

In trying to draw up a Japanese-type aging society based on the basic thoughts listed above, we shall discuss in the following some matters which will become the main supporting pillars of such a society.

(1) Economic Management with Importance Attached to the Prevention of Inflation

In managing the economy, calls will be made for the continued prevention of inflation.

Inflation in the aging society will mean that the aged have difficulty in sustaining self-support as the value of their individual savings kept for old age declines. It will also make it difficult to maintain steady management of the pension system. It will increase anxiety in the aged household without any means of earning income. Needless to say, the prevention of inflation is always an important policy subject. Its importance becomes more significant as the society ages.

(2) Participation of the Aged in Society

In drawing up designs for a Japanese-type aging society, what is most important of all is to open the way for the aged to make good use of their valuable knowledge and experience and allow them to take part in social activities. For this purpose, it is necessary for us to preserve a place for them to positively participate in society by attempting to adjust the supply and demand of labor from multiple angles in future.

[The Significance of the Scenario on Aged Employment]

Based on the present situation of a relatively high ratio of aged labor, a number of selective ways (scenarios) present themselves to us.

One is the early retirement of the aged while the other is employment of the aged.

The latter does not judge that it is fundamentally better not to work, but rather that it should give those who have the ability and will the opportunity to work, thus making good positive use of a diversified sense of values in the substantiation of self-realization that is associated with work itself, and the preservation of social solidarity. This scenario aimed at opening the way for the aged to find work is very significant, especially when we see the difficult reality Western European society is confronted with by opting for the former scenario, which has resulted in increases in the official burden of the welfare society and a decline in wage earners' desire to work.

In the case of Japan, there is a strong desire among the aged to work. Thus, the conditions are complete for the nation to pick the scenario favoring their employment.

[The Establishment of a Labor Market Structure Open to the Aged]

In order to bring about the scenario in favor of the aged, it is necessary for the country to establish a labor market opening its door to old people by trying to work out a variety of responsive measures within the labor market, which, as mentioned previously, is aging fast.

With respect to these points, attempts have been made in the internal labor market to extend the compulsory retirement age and adopt a re-employment system or an employment extension system. However, further endeavors may be called for, such as the completion of educational and training opportunities conforming to the aging progress of society and the development of diversified types and forms of occupation geared to the physical power and intention to work of the aged.

[The Maintenance of Opportunities for Diversified Social Participation]

It is important for healthy old people to participate in wide ranging social activities not only for the sake of making good use of their knowledge and experience but also for the maintenance of their reason to live. For this purpose, attempts should be made to preserve places and opportunities for the aged to engage in diversified work not directly related to employment or income, to complete conditions for old people to join in volunteer or community activities and establish a system of giving them proper appreciation, and to expand chances for them to participate in life long education and leisure or cultural activities in response to their diversified demands.

Also, it may be necessary to promote ways to make use of their rich experience and skill in the form of technical guidance to developing countries.

(3)  Maintenance of Efficient and Proper Welfare

Amid the aging process of society, there will be increased demand for the welfare of the aged, such as the guarantee of income and the preservation of health. In order to preserve economic and social vitality under the conditions of medium growth of the nation's economy, it is necessary to maintain adequate welfare programs by making clear the relationship between proper payments and burden sharing with the consensus of the people.

[The Reform of the Public Pension System]
The public pension system is based on an income guarantee for those in old age, and is therefore designed to contribute to the stability of the Japanese people's old age. It is fundamentally important for the nation to maintain an appropriate pension system for the aging society.

However as seen previously, it is necessary to improve the present public pension system at an early date, because if it is kept without change it will find itself lacking in balance between those who receive pensions and those who pay to support it, between generations. Particularly in the case of revision of the public pension system, it is necessary to consider some measures for those who have already been participating in the program. It is because of this that a long time will be necessary before the effect of any revision becomes visible. Attention, therefore, must be paid to the fact that efforts to revise the present system should be made now, even though the aforementioned problem may not become conspicuous until either the end of the 20th century or the 21st century. Attempts should be made to achieve a proper balance between those who receive the benefits and those who provide the funds, in order for the public pension program to be able to carry out its sound role over a long people on the basis of the solidarity of the Japanese people. Measures considered necessary in revising the existing program include the following: (1) Concerning the standard of payment, a proper level should be set by taking into account differences in the number of dependents, in the structure of consumption and saving and the degree of cost sharing between the pension receiving household and working household; (2) Efforts must be made to correct any imbalance between households or between systems. Drastic reform measures should be discussed, like unifying various pension programs in the years to come; (3) Discussion on gradually raising the eligible age for people to start receiving the pension should happen; (4) Studies should also be made on systematically raising the amount of burden sharing to the level of pension payments as soon as possible.

Still, it is necessary to preserve coordination between such matters as employment, work and income guarantee in dealing with the reform of the public pension system.

[Establishment of a System for the Preservation of Health and Medical Treatment]

In preserving health in old age, it is most important for those who are of advanced age to realize that they must protect their own health and indeed strive to remain in good health. However, in helping them, it is necessary to promote health education at an early date, to establish a health management system and positively promote the people's health building efforts.

Also, it is necessary for administrative organs and related organizations to cooperate in the establishment of a comprehensive health and medical treatment system ranging from the prevention of epidemics to treatment and rehabilitation, and promote such a system in areas which are closely connected with the people's lives. At that time, it will be necessary to pay full attention to both the efficient use of resources for medical care and allotment of welfare services, and move ahead with the priority of the efficient use of medical expenses while sustaining the level of medical care services.

[Formulation of a System to Accommodate Welfare Needs]

The foundation of welfare for the aged is believed to be in the home, but there are cases in which the home alone is not enough to respond to such needs, starting with the extending of care to old people who need it. Therefore, efforts must be made to substantiate welfare services for aged people staying at home and requiring care, as well as placing emphasis on the completing of facilities for the aged in need of care. At that time, it will be necessary for both public and private sectors to cooperate in offering welfare services, strive for the establishment of a system to accommodate the welfare needs of the aged and seek appropriate cost sharing.

[The Practical Use of Private Sector Originality]

It is believed that as diversified welfare services expand in connection with the aging trend, there will be more room for the practical application of the originality of private enterprises.

For example, in connection with the increased demand for welfare services, enterprises operating pay homes for the aged, and free-charging home-help services, may find themselves offering high quality diversified service resulting from technical advance.

[The General Accommodation of Aged Lifestyles]

In considering the lives of the aged from the standpoint of life cycle, there will be a change in the priority of their needs, including employment, pensions, medical treatment and welfare service. That is to say, the maintenance of opportunities to work will serve as the basis for people aged 55-64, while it is expected that for people aged 65-74 the importance of the pension as an income guarantee will increase. Simultaneously, the needs for medical care and welfare will also rise. Generally, it is also expected that the question of welfare for people aged 75 or over will become a central issue. Also, the hookup of medical treatment to welfare will become important. Thus, cooperation will be necessary between all those concerned with the implementation of policies (individuals, homes, enterprises, regional communities, local governments and the central government) to further strengthen their mutual complementary relations and carry out general welfare services, by taking into consideration changes in the important stages of life when accommodating old age lifestyles.

[Accommodating the Handicapped and Their Families]

It is necessary to promote the handicapped's participation in society and try to ease the load off their families in order to establish a society in which they can live and be active as members.

To achieve this, there is a further positive need for preventing the occurrence of diseases, the early discovery of illnesses related to the handicapped, substantial rehabilitation programs, the dispatch of home helpers, more complete welfare services in caring for the handicapped at home, substantial educational programs in accordance with the different needs of the handicapped, and efforts to develop and maintain opportunities for hiring and keeping in employment those handicapped people who have the will and ability to work.

(4) Formation of a Social Environment Comfortable to Live In for the Aged

It is necessary for us to fix the idea in our heads that our future society will be one in which the aged and the handicapped will live and be active as members, and that such a society will be normal (the so-called idea of normalization). At the same time, it is necessary to form a society in which each member can live at ease.

[The Formation of a Living Environment Coping with the Aging Trend]
It will be necessary to establish a living environment in which the aged, amidst the aging trend, can carry out their roles according to their ability and spend pleasant lives in a satisfactory social context.

The aging trend has thus far progressed in local areas, particularly in farming, mountain and fishing villages. This tendency, however, is expected to take place at a rapid pace in big cities in the 1990s.

It is necessary to pay attention to the possibility of various difficult problems emerging, such as the fact that the aging trend in big cities will not only increase vis-a-vis the number of people involved, but will also include a high ratio of single old people. There will be families relatively unable to offer support to their loved ones because of progress in the trend among the Japanese people to have small families — nuclear families — and there will also be a delay in the establishment of communities.

In big cities, efforts have been made to establish facilities for the young. It will be necessary from now on to create facilities for the aged. It will also be necessary to open the way for the aged to participate in the maintenance and management of public facilities as well as community activities, and enhance their roles in society.

Furthermore, in dealing with the complete provision of social capital in future, the following problems will arise from the standpoint of fulfilling the life cycle of individuals who make up the aging society: (1) completing the foundation permitting the aged to participate and interact; (2) making use of the aged in maintaining and managing social capital; (3) completing city and transportation facilities thus allowing the aged to spend pleasant lives, and (4) completing public facilities for the prevention of epidemics and the maintenance and control of health.

[Measures to Deal with Women's Moves into the Labor Market and Proper Positioning of the Home]

The home is extremely important to the aged for a secure life of retirement, their health and welfare. In an attempt to form a social environment ideal for future living, it will be necessary to correctly position the home in society.

In particular, in connection with increases in the number of aged people, there will be more of them forced to live in bed. Thus, with respect to offering care to them, the role of people caring for the aged at home will become more important. For this purpose, it will be necessary for local government bodies, private welfare organizations, volunteers and private enterprises to join together in the establishment of a system designed to sustain homes in need of care for the aged. At the same time, it will be necessary to give proper social evaluation of child rearing, home education and the care of the aged.

Also, it will be necessary to promote a land policy aimed at pressing for three family generations to live in the same place or for family members to live within easy reach.

Furthermore, in order to cope with women's moves into the labor market, it will be necessary to try to establish equality between men and women in employment opportunities and treatment. Also, in order to respond to women's desires to hold diversified jobs, it will be necessary to form special skills and professions paying particular attention to women, provide a stable, part-time labor market for women, and study and press ahead with the formation of a social framework involving employment practices which make it possible for women to suspend work in case of child birth and child rearing, but enable them to resume work later.

[How People of Various Social Classes Will Cope with the Aging Society]

There is a need for people of each social class to accommodate on many levels the trend towards the aging society. These measures include not only those for the aged but also those for the healthy rearing of the children bound to take responsibility in the next generation. Therefore, it will be necessary for the people to have a full understanding of the aging society. For example, it will be important for them to take a renewed look at various existing systems, customs and ways of thinking, allow the aged to be part of society, and also allow the aged to maintain a posture in which they can live satisfactorily as individuals. Social solidarity among the people of various classes will become more important as we move closer to the aging society.Also, it will be necessary for enterprises to show understanding and cooperation with respect to the maintenance of jobs for the aged.

[Thoughts on Population]
        Here in this chapter, we have dealt with measures to cope with the aging society on the pretext of birth rates, changes in population and the aging trend mentioned in Chapter 2. In the event the birth rate fails to recover and remains low, the difficulty mentioned earlier may further accelerate. However, changes in population movements are decided by economic and systematic factors in many instances. As we consider various problems accompanying the trend towards an aging society in future, it is conceivable that the question of how to move population will probably become a major issue of study.

        Naturally, the issue is related to the way of lifestyles and sense of value, and therefore it is difficult to demonstrate a uniform direction. It is necessary, however, to examine at least whether or not the Japanese economic and social systems are moving towards the promotion of a decline in the birth rate.

        The drop in the birth rate in recent years has stepped up the aging tendency. It is likely to bring about a great effect on the population balance between generations in future. Against this background, it will become more important for us to have children and raise them in good health in preparation for the aging society.

## Section 3    The Maturity of the Economic Society and Maintenance of Vitality

        The third large trend leading to the 21st century is maturity of the economic society. Japan has caught up with other advanced countries. Henceforth, it will move into the stage of maturity in its economic society. What it must pay most attention to in this connection is that the vitality of the economic society, the source of ability to resolve problems, should not be lost, as the dynamism of the economic society weakens in reaching maturity.

## 1. The Maturity of Economic Society and Its Vitality

### (1) The Significance of Maturity and Vitality

[Progress Towards the Maturity of Economic Society]
Japan will reach a stage of maturity after having caught up with other advanced countries, and its economic society will mature in diversified ways.

First, economically, there will be a shift from an economy centered around industrialization and materials to that of knowledge and services (a tendency towards economic softness). In such a situation, there will be more individual and diversified consumption.

Also, in terms of society, there will be a trend away from seeking improvements in income and materialistic satisfaction to a society discovering major value in the field of harmony and latitude under a manifold sense of values. Furthermore, taking into consideration declines in the rate of population increase, progressive aging, the various effects of such a situation as seen in Section 2 may be cited as problems associated with the trend towards the maturity of economic society.

[The Importance of Economic Vitality]
In the midst of the maturing trend of economic society, how we understand economic vitality and look at its future may hold the key to our long-term thinking of the future of our economic society.

It is difficult to strictly define economic vitality. However, the following may be cited as its concrete manifestations.

One is economic growth enabling the pie to increase in size and power. Japan has continued to achieve relatively higher economic growth than the United States and European countries not only during its high growth era between the second half of the 1950s and the latter half of the 1960s but also during the period of its shift to medium growth after the oil crisis. It is possible to believe that the ability to register high economic growth during both medium and long-term periods is a manifestation of economic vitality.

Another is the power to adapt to changes in external conditions. The postwar Japanese economy has undergone a number of changes in external conditions such as the liberalization of trade, the Nixon shock, the revaluation of the yen in relation to the dollar, environmental problems and two oil crises. Whenever such changes came about, there were many people who took pessimistic views of the future of the Japanese economy, but looking at the results of these experiences, they prove that Japan has succeeded in weathering the changes with considerable elasticity. The ability to adapt to change is considered a manifestation of economic vitality.

Of course, these two elements are not independent but rather mutually related. This is because when there is high growth it is easy to absorb the friction generated from changes, while high accommodation makes it possible to maintain relatively high growth in the midst of changes.

[Vitality as the Source of Ability to Resolve Problems]

As it moves on towards the 21st century, Japanese economic society will face many changes and will have to solve difficult problems in the face of such large trends as internationalization and the aging society as seen earlier. In this situation, economic vitality as the power to accommodate the power of growth and changes will become the source of ability to settle problems. To positively maintain and shape such vitality will be a fundamental condition for Japan to resolve various problems in heading for the 21st century.

[The Importance of Social Vitality]

It is important to attach importance not only to the economic aspect but rather more to social vitality.

It is important for all people who make up society to live energetically with spiritual satisfaction, and build a society full of vitality, even though this may not directly relate to productive activities. Just living like this itself is fundamentally important. The importance for society to uphold its vitality in response to a diversified sense of value is rising, particularly since the process of catching up with other advanced nations in pursuit of material affluence has ended, and it has now become difficult to pursue a single goal. For this purpose, it is necessary to have the opportunities for manifold self-realization.

Voluntary social and cultural activities may play important roles in this connection.

Also important as we consider future social vitality is what kind of sense of value the young, brought up in affluent society, will have in the midst of the aging trend, maturity of economic society and internationalization, and to what field they are going to devote their energy. The rising generation, newly participating in society heading for the 21st century, is expected to become the bearer of a vital society with a diversified sense of value.

## (2) Vitality Amidst the Move Towards Maturity

The various elements of economic society which thus far have sustained the vitality of this country will probably undergo gradual changes as the economic society matures. There will be a call for the need to positively maintain and form vitality.

### a. Technical Development

Progress in technical development and its concrete manifestations through investment in facilities are the biggest foundation of economic vitality. As Japan has completed catching up with other advanced countries, it has found it gradually more difficult to uphold its vitality, merely relying on the past practice of realizing technical development based on the introduction and application of technical knowhow.

[New Evolution of Technical Innovation in Demand]
Up to now, Japan has actively brought in technology from industrially advanced countries, such as the United States and those in Western Europe, improved it and continued to strive for development of its own technology. As a result, the technical standard of Japanese industry has reached the world's top level in almost all fields.

Such technical progress has sustained the country's economic growth by helping increase labor and capital productivity and connecting it with the development of new products.

However, technical development under the past "catch-up" formula will gradually become more difficult. Japan must take on creative and innovative technical development, something it has found hard to deal with.

b. Competitive Environment for Individuals and Enterprises

The desire for progress held by individuals and enterprises, and their vitality, are believed to have supported the economic society of this nation. In the midst of the maturing trend of economic society, it is believed that the environment around both individuals and enterprises will undergo changes.

[Past Competitive Environment]
It is believed that there has been an environment encouraging active competition behind the micro-level vitality of individuals and enterprises.

First, on the individual level, there is a fair distribution of income and wealth in Japan. Liquidity among social classes is also high. Therefore, wide, selective ways have remained open for each individual to decide on his or her future. Competition in the educational and professional fields has been maintained. This, in turn, has prompted individuals to study and work hard and make efforts to advance their social status. It is believed that their efforts have sustained the high Japanese desire to work. In other words, an environment featuring reward in return for any endeavor was considered to have generated vitality at the individual level.

Also, at the enterprise level, there has been severe competition between enterprises or within enterprise groups, as attested to by such words as "excessive competition." Thus, the propagation of technical innovation within industry has been very rapid. It is believed that there has been an atmosphere allowing Japanese industry to improve product quality and workers to engage either in creative work or devising products at their places of work.

[Maturity and the Competitive Environment]
However, it is considered possible that such a competitive environment at the individual and enterprise level will gradually change in the wake of moves towards the maturity of economic society.

First, it is believed that as the income level increases and the sense of value diversifies, the people's desire to raise their living standards and social status will wane.

Second, as seen in Section 2, there would be a loss of balance between those who receive welfare benefits and those who must shoulder the welfare program between generations, if we fail to take proper measures in coping with the aging society. There is a fear that this could obstruct vitality at the individual level.

Third, amid the aging of the labor force, dissemination of higher education, and shift to medium growth, it is possible that there will be stagnation in the field of organization within enterprises, and management may find it difficult to give employees promotions and provide other incentives.

Fourth, it is possible that as the country's economy shifts to medium growth and the tempo of enterprises' market expansion slows down, there will be moves by corporate firms to resort to cooperative actions and monopolies.

### c.  Labor Productivity

A manifestation of macro-vitality is the rise in productivity. Thus far, Japan has developed its economy by increasing labor productivity. However, from now on, it will gradually become difficult for the nation to continue to maintain macro productivity. This is due to the fact that it has fundamentally completed its process of catching up with other industrially advanced countries and will witness a move towards the maturity of its economic society.

[The Increase in the Services Industry]
The following can be considered as factors contributing to a slowdown in the rate of growth in macro-productivity.

First, it is likely that the services industry, which has relatively low productivity increases, will gain in importance. In connection with the future maturity of consumption, it is believed possible that there will be increases in demand for service activities. However, since the services industry aimed at individuals is a field which shows relatively slow increases in productivity, it will move in the direction of a slowdown in the ratio of growth in labor productivity.

[Changes in Composition of the Labor Force]

Second, the composition of the labor force centering on the young will rise to one relatively composed of old people.

A young work force maintains strong adaptability to changes because it is not closely associated with existing technology and knowhow. However, with increases in the labor force comprising more older people, there will be an increasing need to offer them educational training. Unless there are moves to cope properly with these changes, it is possible that there will be a slowdown in the rate of growth in productivity.

## d. Enterprise Organization, Employment Practices

Japanese enterprises have played the role of vitality promoters by combining the effectiveness of management resources under organizational aspects unique to this country. But, slowly, they are being asked to adopt new countermeasures.

[The Role of Japanese Employment Practices]

It is believed that Japan's characteristic employment practices used by corporate firms centering around the major enterprises — such as life employment, wages based on seniority, assignments and job-switching within enterprises with the education necessary to carry them out — is a system making good use of the internal labor market function by upholding the principle of selecting employees from within and giving them promotions.

Under this practice, workers have gained the satisfaction of their desire to enhance their lives with the wages they have received under the seniority system compatible with their life cycle. Simultaneously, through the promotion system and educational training, workers have been satisfied with the realization of their self-desires and increased their working desire.

Also, through job training and smooth changes in the place of work within enterprises, it has become possible for companies to positively cope with technical innovations and demonstrate a high level of adaptability to change.

Furthermore, the closed enterprise labor unions, established to keep close contact with the labor market within corporate firms, have made it possible for labor and management to maintain close communications. At the same time, they have succeeded in realizing the maximum enhancement of wage and labor conditions suitable to the ability of the enterprise.

[The Role of Japanese Style Management]
The organization of the Japanese enterprise has special characteristics in that it has considerable transfers of power in the fields of administration and management, while it depends to a large extent on the creative work of laborers in the actual business operation. Such Japanese-style management has made it possible to create favorable management-labor relations, cope flexibly with culture, and establish management goals and decide management's long-term desires.

At the same time, Japan's unique indirect monetary system has sustained demand for the capital necessary for investment in facilities. Banks and corporate firms have also joined together in supporting the foundation for long term growth under the main bank system.

[Changes in the Environment Concerning Enterprise Organization and Employment Practices]
Looking at the prospects for the 21st century, it is expected that corporate firms and their employment practices will be confronted with such changes as (1) a slowdown in the tempo of market expansion and market maturity, (2) progress in technical innovation, (3) a slowdown in the growth of the number of people of productive age, the trend towards an aging labor force and the trend towards people with higher education, (4) changes in worker consciousness and the diversification of sense of value, (5) internationalization of business development, and (6) a diversified and liberalized money market.

In the midst of this situation, Japanese-style management will probably retain the basic framework of its employment practices. But it is considered that there will be calls for a partial change. It will probably be necessary to devise new countermeasures to maintain and organize vitality in response to calls for an appropriate evaluation of its role.

## 2. Basic Strategy for the Maintenance and Formation of Vitality

As we have seen thus far, the maintenance and formation of vitality in the maturing process will become an increasingly important issue. If anyone neglects to cope with these changes and contents themselves with the old existing system and customs, they will see both a gradual decline in vitality and an increasing fear of the emergence of a sluggish economic society lacking in the power to achieve economic growth. It is necessary for us to maintain a posture of not only maintaining vitality but also of constantly organizing vitality in the midst of change.

### (1)　The Maintenance of Affluent Creativity

In the maturing process of the so-called "post catch up" era, Japan will enter an era without any precedents in many fields. In this situation, it will be necessary for this nation to open up its own creative sources for the maintenance and formation of vitality for its economic society.

[The Promotion of Creative Technical Development]

It will be necessary for Japan to not only continue the development of technological application and improvements in future, but also move ahead with the development of creative and individualistic technology. There will be a considerable risk of failure in such endeavors in the creative field, but Japan must move ahead with the development of technology in response to the needs of society centering around technology in tune with the national situation. Also, any future scientific technology must been close relation to the social and human sciences. It will also be necessary to pay further attention to the effects on human society, the natural environment and their harmony. In this sense, it will be important to carry out research in inter-disciplinary territory.

It will be necessary for this country to try to expand the scope of investment in research and development, substantiate the field of basic research as the foundation to support its development, to step up the promotion of scientific education, grasp the needs of the people, discover and nurture the technology necessary for development, and apply practically already developed technology and make use of it for commercial ventures, all for the sake of sustaining development. The government needs to come up with positive measures for this purpose.

In the area of the labor market too, conditions must be prepared so as to make it possible to cope positively with technological innovation.

[Training Creative Personnel]

In order to maintain the affluent creativity of technical development and other areas, it is necessary for the nation to train those rich in creativity.

For this purpose, it is requested that measures be taken to activate its educational system centering around the universities by strengthening internationalization and research incentives.

In particular, in view of changes in the population, there will be an increasing need to enhance individual creativity. This will be necessary in order to countervail the current of changes seen in a relative decline of the ratio of those below the age of 35 said to be highly creative.

[The Construction of a Creative Economic Social System]

In the past, Japan frequently took methods of learning from other nations in building its own economic and social systems and worked them out on the basis of what it found from others.

However, within the maturing process, Japan finds itself without any previous example in the maintenance of vitality. The upshot of this is a matter of creative challenge without parallel, and we must respond to it with our own hands.

(2)   The Replenishment of Environmental Vitality

The vitality of Japanese economic society has been sustained by free and competitive activities based on creativity and contrivance in the private sector. It is believed that this will remain unchanged in future. Therefore, it will be necessary to replenish the environment (vital environment) allowing the private sector to display its full vitality for the maintenance and formation of vigor within the maturing process.

[The Formation of the Appropriate Social Framework]

First, full provision of environmental vitality means providing a social framework with incentives for the private sector to demonstrate its energy sufficiently.

For this purpose, it will be necessary to construct a society establishing a clear correlation between efforts and results, cause and effect, those receiving benefits and those shouldering the burden, and earnings and costs; a society maintaining opportunities for equality so that flourishing entrepreneurs and enterprising individuals can fully demonstrate their worth.

[The Maintenance of an Enterprise Competitive Environment]

Second, an enterprise competitive environment must be maintained.

The provision of competitive conditions to induce the full vitality of private firms will become an increasingly important issue as the tempo of market expansion becomes sluggish under medium economic growth.

In this instance, consideration must be given to the maintenance of competitive conditions in the midst of global expansion as internationalization proceeds. In particular, it will be necessary to pay sufficient attention to prevent protectionist tendencies when domestic industry is exposed to severe competition through the expansion of imports of manufactured goods in future.

[An Appropriate Economic Policy]

Third, the government must implement appropriate economic policies so as to prevent stagflation and guide the vitality of the private sector to a favorable macro-performance.

To achieve this, it must put various policies into practice for the suitable control of general demand, money supply management, technical development from a medium- and long-term standpoint, and for the enhancement of small and medium enterprises, the agricultural industry and the monetary market.

[An Appropriate Evaluation of Japanese-Style Management and Employment Practices]

Fourth, there is the question of both giving a proper evaluation of and fixing the position of Japanese-style management and employment practices.

Japanese-style management and employment practices will gradually be forced to undergo changes as the economic society matures and internationalization progresses. However, enough attention ought to be paid to those aspects which served as the foundation for the vitality of Japanese economic society in the past. And, we must give them due evaluation and try to fix their position.

Also, new devices will become necessary, not only to uphold the existing system, but to boost the function of top management, redesign the job classification system including skill evaluation, substantiate the development of employee capacity and expand job areas for old people and women in response to changes in the environment.

[Future Countermeasures for Small Businesses]

Fifth, small businesses, too, must try to come up with new measures to cope with future development.

Small businesses, which account for the bulk of Japanese industry, have played major roles in the development of the Japanese economic society. Whether they can cope with changes in industrial society or not will be the key to whether Japanese industrial society can create new vitality or not.

For this purpose, it will be necessary for small and medium industries themselves to take appropriate measures such as switches in management strategy from quantity to quality, efforts towards a greater display of creativity and mobility, and to support these, they must adopt measures to promote what can be expanded as well as suitable measures to deal with changes in the industrial structure.

[Maintenance of the Foundation for Social Vitality]

Sixth, it will be necessary to complete the foundation for maintaining and forming social vitality.

For this purpose, it will be necessary to enrich opportunities for self-realization, and maintain high social liquidity and the equality of individual opportunity.

It will also be necessary to fully prepare the basis for including wide ranging cultural activities among educational activities and cultural facilities. Furthermore, it will be important to maintain and form social vitality in order to (1) expand the opportunities and forums for life-long education given the recent strong tendency for life-long education and study in recent years, and (2) make it possible for many people to have easy access to opportunities for diversified self-realization through various means such as freedom of the right to choose one's place of residence, expansion of the scope of activity and the obtaining of advanced information.

## Section 4    Problems Common to the Three Large Trends

We have up to now dealt with the basic strategy and questions needed to cope with "internationalizations," "the aging society" and the "maturity" of economic society. However, there are problems common to these three large trends. In the following, we shall discuss what we consider the main problems to be, such as "efforts to guarantee a safe economic society," "the formation of high quality national land and living space," and "the role of the public sector and appropriate countermeasures."

### 1.   Efforts to Guarantee a Safe Economic Society

It is believed that the question of a safe economic society means "protecting economic activities which serve as the foundation of our society from threats from outside the economic system." It is expected that in moving towards the 21st century Japan will deepen its international mutual dependence, accelerating the importance of the issue of the safety of economic society. As stated in Chapter 2, based on the pretext of future prospects, a steady supply of resources, energy and foodstuffs — subjects which became an issue in the 1970s — will continue to be a major problem for the safety of economic society. Also, preparation for maritime transportation of these important items, and for a large-scale earthquake which could be a domestic threat, will be a question which should not be neglected. It will be necessary to cope with these matters appropriately so that any possibility of the occurrence of a crisis or damage in the event that such a crisis did occur can be held to a minimum.

## (1)  Multiple Safety Measures

As a measure of the safety of economic society, it will be necessary to build a multiple safety device combining a number of stages and means for countermeasures. The following three stages exist as means to deal with a crisis, but each countermeasure at each level must be put forward in a complex way.

[Foreknowledge and Prevention of the Occurrence of a Crisis]
Firstly, there are the foreknowledge of and prevention of the occurrence of any crisis.

In the present internationalization process, it is not possible for Japan to seek self-sufficiency in safety. It must pursue safety under international mutual dependence. As Japan has become a major economic power, there have been increases in both the possibility and need for it to offer contributions in the fields of crisis foreknowledge and prevention, under international cooperation. With respect to the question of knowing beforehand about a crisis, it is important for Japan to make an accurate analysis of the international oil situation and obtain at an early date information on the situation of the global grain crop. As for endeavors to prevent a crisis, it is the duty of Japan as a major economic power to positively contribute to the stability and development of the international community. At the same time, it is important for this nation — a strong economic power and big consumer — to cooperate with the developing nations in the development of agricultural, forestry and fisheries industries as well as the development of oil for the improvement of global supply and demand. This is because the suppressed worldwide supply and demand in resources, energy and foodstuffs can easily lead to a crisis.

[Overcoming the Inability to Deal with a Crisis]
Secondly, efforts must be made to conquer the inability to cope with a crisis.

This means that Japan should strive to reinforce its constitution in advance so that, upon the occurrence of a crisis, it can keep the damage to its economy at a minimum. Concerning energy, diversification of its supply, the promotion of energy-saving measures and a full stock-piling of oil will become important pillars. It is also necessary for the country to press ahead with measures to seek a steady supply and the maintenance, including stockpiling, of non-energy mineral resources. As for foodstuffs, it is important for Japan to effectively develop domestic production on the basis of the efficient use of domestic resources, such as farm land, with high productivity and fishing grounds, and try to maintain and strengthen self-sustenance in food. At the same time, it must cooperate with others in the formation of an order in the international agricultural market. It is also important for it to try to maintain steady imports through bilateral agreements and the establishment of multiple sources of imports. Regarding lumber, it is important for the country to cultivate and maintain domestic forest resources and boost the domestic production system in order to minimize declines in the world's forest resources, which are being forecast over a long period. Furthermore, the nation must make further efforts in bringing up the ratio of Japanese flag carriers in maritime transportation and in preventive measures against major earthquakes.

[Countermeasures for the Occurrence of a Crisis]

Thirdly, countermeasures are needed at the time of crisis occurrence.

It is particularly important for the nation in this aspect to maintain a system of obtaining energy-related information, to maintain communicational functions at the time of the occurrence of an earthquake, to maintain the distribution of accurate information and prepare in advance a proper information management system. This will help prevent panic and be useful in taking quick measures to control a crisis. Also, there must be a need for it to establish a standard for the amounts to be taken out of stockpiles of oil and foodstuffs and a formula for their distribution. It also must try to incorporate the capacity for expansion of the volume of domestic food supply into the normal production system so that a switch can be made in domestic agricultural output in case of an emergency.

For the safety of economic society, these countermeasures at each level must be adopted in a complex way. At that time, study will be needed from the standpoint of cost effectiveness so as to check for any conspicuous damage to the efficiency of the economy as a whole. Also, as Japan has become a major economic power, it is conceivable that the cost it must bear will increase. Such a safety cost, in the final analysis, is a burden shouldered by the people. It is important for the country to raise the people's consciousness such that in order to increase the safety of economic society they must shoulder the cost burden appropriately.

(2)  The Study of Safety Standards from the Standpoint of National Life

Also, in pushing ahead with the promotion of measures for the safety of the future economic society, it is necessary to seize upon the question of the safety of economic society not just from the standpoint of the economy of one nation but also from the visual point of the people's daily lives. In other words, it is necessary to consider a safety standard — a sort of minimum security (for the stability of national life) — to prevent any serious obstacle arising from any external or domestic crisis of any degree, and study whether such a standard is actually incorporated into the general economic social system. It is expected that moving ahead with this kind of measure will enable the nation to avoid any further serious social disorder such as the one generated by the first oil crisis. In order to pursue this minimum security, much more discussion will be necessary on the standard for the minimum, the scope of goods to be made subject to it and the system's function. It is hoped that debates and study on this matter will take place in various circles, taking the examples of other countries into account.

## 2.  The Formation of High Quality National Land and Living Space

(1)  The Realization of a Comfortable and Open Society for Permanent Settlement

[Diversified Choices for Settlement and the Urbanization Trend]
As stated in Chapter 2, it is expected that the people's intention to settle down will continue as we move into the 21st century. In the midst of this situation, diversified population movements are likely to take place as those born in the second postwar baby boom get older and move from place to place to seek higher education, while others shift from one place to another to choose their jobs, because of the trend for higher education and a service economy. Still, there will be

those people who will probably move away from the cities, where they settled during the era of high economic growth, to other places to live in retirement.

In addition to these movements, it is expected that the next 20-30 years will provide the last stages for the large-scale urbanization of Japanaese towns and cities. This is because the population of Japan is likely to continue to grow for some time in future and that rises in the ratio of secondary and tertiary industries will reflect on such urbanization moves.

Also, as seen in Section 1 of this chapter, internationalization will take place not only in big cities alone but also in bloc-centered cities. With their international functions likely to be intensified, it is possible that internationalization will make progress even when it is regarded as a regional thing.

[The Doctrine of a Comfortable and Open Society for Permanent Settlement]

Keeping the above-mentioned tendency in mind, it is necessary for us to aim for the realization of the following land and living space measures as we move towards the 21st century. They are (1) the wider use of limited available land: (2) the fact that various areas must make use of their own characteristics and special features as well as be equipped with an affluent living environment and diversified steady employment opportunities: (3) the emergence of an open society for permanent settlement, guaranteeing anyone living in any part of the nation the possibility to live a pleasant life while giving others who still seek a life worth living more in other places higher mobility.

[The Formation of a Regional Society with High Mobility]

In the midst of the continued tendency for people seeking permanent settlement in places they have picked, regional society should not become immobile and closed. The people must be guaranteed easy access to opportunities for high level and diversified self-realization. There is a need to form open regional societies not only in Japan but in overseas countries as well. And, high mobility must be guaranteed in the fields of transportation and information as well as residential movements.

For this purpose, it will be necessary for local areas in Japan to try and organize local societies featuring their own respective functions and attractions in order to cope with the diversified choice of places for residence in future.

Also, it will be necessary to allow people settling permanently to enjoy varied opportunities in response to their needs. Regarding transportation, mobility must be maintained for those areas located far from any axis of the superexpress road system. Also attempts should be made to dissolve any gap in the means of obtaining information on transportation between big cities and local regions, particularly in connection with the transportation systems adopted by local regions to cope with increased urbanization of the city peripheries. Furthermore, there is a need for local communities to expand the opportunities available for high level as well as life long education.

[A Method for the Regional Economy to Achieve Independent Development]

The economies of local Japanese areas are likely to lag far behind the big cities if they continue under the present situation because they depend largely on financial transfers (local grant taxes and investments in public works projects) and the foundation for their independent growth is weak. Also, there are not enough chances for young men and women to take on advanced and diversified jobs which could induce them to settle down.

In order to reinforce the constitution of such local economies and let them accomplish their own independent development, it will be necessary to (1) strengthen the central management functions of bloc-centered cities and also build up their international functions: (2) promote high technology industry located factories in local areas: (3) give local industry high added value by intensifying its technical, commercial and planning power: (4) form a high yielding agricultural industry and bring up industry making good use of resources and agricultural, forestry and fishery products unique to local areas.

[A Method to Provide Urban Community Zones]

As for existing urban districts in the hearts of urban communities, it will be important to promote advanced land-use, improve their safety in the event of natural calamities and try to change the residential environment for the better.

For this purpose, it will be necessary to (1) move ahead with the intense use of residential areas which account for the bulk of existing urban districts and make them into new, favorable urban community residential districts, bringing residential areas and places of work close together: (2) carry out redevelopment of city areas with importance attached to those areas with a worsening environment and economically declining areas which are likely to further deteriorate in future. Particularly bad residential structures should be rebuilt while close attention must be paid to the provision of public facilities in implementing city redevelopment programs: (3) either build or repair facilities on the condition, as stated in Section 3, that they be used by the aged.

As for peripheral areas, it will be necessary to carry out systematic city building plans designed to prevent city sprawling and random development. It will be important for such areas to try to multi-nuclearize and widen their available space, much like the construction of urban zones. For this purpose it will be necessary for them to retain in advance high quality open public space, which will become the framework of future city building, and build both nucleus cities and others surrounding them.

[A Method to Outfit Local Cities, Farming, Mountain and Fishing Villages]

Provincial cities, especially central cities in local areas, will rapidly urbanize. It will be important for them not to invite the formation of deteriorated city districts due to a delay in measures to cope with them. Therefore, it will be necessary to renovate areas within the cities from the long-term standpoint of investment effectiveness and make full preparations for the foundation of such reforms ahead of time. City districts must be distributed systematically and in such a way as to maintain harmony between agricultural space and green zones. The construction of cities must be made by coping with the progress of motorization.

A city-like life pattern is expected to spread in future to mountain, farming and fishing villages. They will also become places with a mixture of farmer-fishermen households and residences for non-farmers and non-fishermen. The mountain, farming and fishing villages will not only provide productive space but also living space for residents. They will also maintain their functions as national land preserves, recreational areas and places for the people to recover their humanity. Thus, it will be necessary to maintain and accelerate such features and fully provide the conditions for permanent settlement. For this purpose, there is a need to complete the foundation for production, prepare united environmental facilities and improve the living environment. Also, it will be necessary to try to bring those industries making use of local resources into the area and guarantee job opportunities.

Furthermore, it will be necessary for the residents of urban communities and villages to be able to appreciate their respective good points. To achieve this, moves must be made towards the formation of an organic, united living zone between urban communities and villages.

[A Method for Providing Houses]
The demand for new houses will slow down in the long run because of a sluggish increase in the number of households and reduced population movements to big cities. However, with rises in the income level and the diversification of sense of values and consciousness, there appear to be strong needs for improvements in the quality of houses, including the housing environment. Also, it is expected that the form of home living will diversify given the country's aging trend, involving the question of having three generations of the same family under the same roof, or the families of grandparents, parents and children living in different houses located close to each other. Therefore, in providing homes in future, it will be necessary to (1) attach importance to public assistance in connection with the building of new homes and reinforce city planning restrictions to induce the construction of better quality houses: (2) promote in the cities a supply of communal housing areas for high level use and the construction of privately managed homes meeting a fixed living standard: (3) promote the smooth distribution of existing housing stocks and establish living rules concerning the maintenance and management of medium and high rise communal housing facilities which are rapidly rising in number: (4) promote the participation and cooperation of landowners in the supply of land for housing construction and work towards raising the desire of private housing businessmen to share the burden of the housing business fairly. And, especially in large urban communities, attempts should be made

to promote the effective and appropriate use of land and switch the land available for the building of houses with the strengthening of restrictions on the use of land and realization of proper costs for the possession of land.

(2) The Formation of a High Quality and Stable National Land Foundation

The buildup in social capital has made steady progress from the standpoint of dissolving bottlenecks in economic growth and enhancing Japanese national life. The level of buildup has therefore been raised considerably with the stock increasing by about seven times in the past 20 years.

However, the buildup in social capital has not fully coped with the rapid progress in urbanization. As a result, the quality of Japanese living space has remained at a low level. In terms of the standard of buildup of social capital, Japan is generally lower than America and the advanced countries of Western Europe (See Table 3-4-1). It will be necessary for Japan to continue to build up its social capital steadily and systematically.

[The Accumulation of Quality Stock]

In the past, Japan was inclined to pursue short-term effectiveness in building up its social capital. However, in future, it must pay attention to having facilities rich in capacity to withstand the changes of the times, their harmony with the natural environment and regional society and easy maintenance and management. It will also be necessary for the country to steadily build up quality stocks which can be maintained effectively for a long period. At that time, it will be necessary to improve the existing system and the means for the strengthening of public control on the effective use of land, and promote the full preparation of the environment on the basis of the creativity of regional people and private bodies, together with the buildup of social capital.

The buildup in social capital in proceeding to the 21st century must progress with the considerations mentioned above in mind. At the same time, it will be necessary for Japan to cope with the aging society, the move towards urbanization, internationalization and information,

# Table 3-4-1 An International Comparison of the Level of Buildup in Social Capital

| Division | Unit | Japan | Britain | W. Germany | France | Italy | U.S. |
|---|---|---|---|---|---|---|---|
| City parks | | | | | | | |
| Size of land per person | m²/person | (1976) 3.5 | (1976) London 30.4 | (1973) Bon 26.9 | (1973) Paris 8.4 | (1973) Rome 11.4 | (1976) Washington, D.C. 45.7 |
| Sewerage | | | | | | | |
| Rate of diffusion per total population | % | (1977) 26 | (1976) 97 | (1977) 88 | (1975) 65 | ( — ) — | (1968) 71 |
| Housing | | | | | | | |
| Average number of rooms per house | room/household | (1978) 4.5 | (1971) 4.9 | (1978) 4.9 | (1978) 3.8 | (1977) 4.1 | (1976) 5.1 |
| Average number of persons per room | person/room | (1978) 0.8 | (1971) 0.6 | (1976) 0.6 | (1973) 0.8 | (1971) 0.9 | (1970) 0.6 |
| Roads | | | | | | | |
| Rate of road paving | % | (1980) 16 [48] | (1979) 96 | (1979) 97 | (1979) 92 | (1979) 93 | (1978) 52 |
| Length of paved roads per unit of automobile | m/unit | (1979) 5.0 | (1978) 21.3 | (1978) 20.0 | (1978) 36.5 | (1978) 15.4 | (1977) 21.8 |
| Length of expressways | km | (1980.3) 2,579 | (1979.4) 2,416 | (end of 1979) 7,292 | (end of 1979) 4,896 | (end of 1979) 5,822 | (end of 1978) 81,700 |
| Railways | | | | | | | |
| Rate of national railway double tracks | % | (1977) 25.7 | (1977) 70.8 | (1977) 42.8 | (1977) 44.5 | (1977) 32.4 | ( — ) — |
| Waterworks | | | | | | | |
| Diffusion rate | % | (1977) 89.4 | (1961) 99.0 | (1963) 91.0 | (1962) 79.0 | ( — ) — | (1960) 93.0 |

| | | | | | | | |
|---|---|---|---|---|---|---|---|
| Medical service | | | | | | | |
| Number of hospital beds per 10,000 people | bed/10,000 persons | (1978) 107.1 | (1975) 89.9 | (1975) 118.0 | (—) — | (1972) 105.8 | (1975) 65.6 |
| Telephones Diffusion rate | number/ 100 persons | (1978.1) 42.4 | (1978.1) 41.5 | (1978.1) 37.4 | (1978.1) 32.9 | (1978.1) 28.5 | (1978.1) 74.4 |

**Notes:** Sources of reference materials are as follows:

City parks, sewerage: Studies made by the Ministry of Construction.

Housing (Average number of rooms per house): Information on Japanese rooms from "1978 housing statistics survey" by the Statistics Bureau of the Prime Minister's Office; those on Britain and the U.S. from studies made by the Construction Ministry; those on West Germany and France from "Annual Bulletin of Housing and Building Statistics for Europe." Incidentally, not included are rooms smaller than 6 m² in West Germany and those smaller than 9 m² and kitchens in France.

(Average number of people per room): Japan's information came from "1978 housing statistics survey" by the Statistics Bureau of the Prime Minister's Office. Those on other countries from the "1979 White Paper on Construction."

Roads: Japanese roads, from reference material of the Construction Ministry. Those in other countries from IRF statistics. Rate of road paving and length of paved roads per unit of automobile: The figures are the numerical value of roads covering cities, towns and villages of all the countries listed in the table. Also ( ) in Japan represent the numerical value of the national highways as well as prefectural highways.

Railways: Information on Japan, from reference material of the Ministry of Construction; those in other countries from U.I.C. reference material.

Waterworks: From surveys of the Water Supply and Environmental Sanitation Department of the Ministry of Health and Welfare.

Telephones: From "Illustrated Telegraph and Telephone Service" (January 1980) by the Japan Telegraph and Telephone Public Corporation.

— 169 —

as Japan is expected to see a change in that direction in its economic society. Especially since Japan is going to see large-scale urbanization, which may be the last of its kind in the next 20-30 years, it will be necessary for the nation to strive to build up a pleasant urban living environment. The following is what the buildup in social capital should be, as we divide it into: (1) the foundation for protecting national life and the safety of society (safety base), (2) the foundation for the maintenance of the vitality of economic society (base for vitality), and (3) the foundation for the realization of pleasant national life (base for pleasant life). At that time, it will be necessary, in fully providing a living environment, to improve safety for large urban communities, raise the level of pleasant living conditions in the vicinity of urban communities and attach importance to active regions in local areas.

[The Buildup of the Safety Base]

(1) Efforts must be made to seek further improvements in safety for the preservation of national land facilities, in coping with the fragility of national land. National land resources such as forests and water must be preserved and a system should be created to maintain such resources on a steady basis. (2) A system ought to be established to renovate urban communities to enhance their safety against major earthquakes and fire; facilities must be completed to sustain safe transportaion; endeavors should be made to correct the weakness which tends to prompt central management functions to concentrate in Tokyo; and efforts should be made to set up a system which will enable trunk transportation and communication networks to operate even with the occurrence of natural disasters. (3) As for energy, attempts should be made to complete the foundation of facilities for the development and effective use of energy stockpiles and imports, and of alternative energy sources. Also, attempts should be made to establish stable domestic food production, and maintain a system which can cope flexibly with the occurrence of crises.

[Providing a Base for Vitality]

(1) Attempts should be made to establish a system for a high speed transportation network, a regional transportation network and the completion of facilities for the distribution of goods as well as advanced information and communications systems on a balanced and

efficient scale covering the entire nation. (2) Efforts should be made to acquire smoothly and ahead of time the land needed for high technology industry whose demand is expected in future, and supply facilities. Preparation for completing the base for the research and development of technology on alternative energy sources and energy saving, should also be made. (3) There should be endeavors to substantiate the educational and academic facilities needed to foster people rich in creativity and humanity.

[The Basis for a Pleasant Life]
In making good use of the culture, natural environment and special features available in urban communities and local areas, it will be necessary to (1) enrich environmental hygiene and press ahead with undertakings on the completion of the foundation of an environment providing the people with a healthy and comfortable life: (2) build up the basis for the formation of affluent and cultural human beings: (3) fully prepare for the foundation of an affluent and tasteful living environment: (4) build up transportation and communications facilities in support of the people's daily lives. In doing so, it will also be necessary to try to promote the provision of space to cope with urbanization in the local sphere which is likely to progress at a rapid pace in future.

[Balanced Public Investment]
In moving ahead with future efforts to build up social capital, attention must be paid to maintaining the balance between public and private investment from both a medium- and long-term point of view so that there will be no relative excess or deficiency in such investment. It will also be necessary to make steady progress in building up the living environment.

Also, it will be necessary to find investment opportunities proportionate to the people's saving deposits. As stated in Chapter 2, regarding this point, it is believed that there will not be any large absorption of excess household savings in the form of large scale excess private enterprise investments which took place during the era of high economic growth in Japan It will be necessary to pay full attention to the effect on the household savings rate brought about by future movements in the reform of the social security system, as well as changes in living customs and other main factors. It will also be necessary to direct the nation's economic power towards the formation of a good quality land foundation, carry out balanced public investment, and accumulate social capital on a systematic and steady basis in preparation for the coming aging society of the 21st century.

[A Renewed Look at Social Capital Services and the Effectiveness of Their Buildup]

It is necessary to always take renewed looks at the buildup in social capital carried out by the public sector, as changes take place according to the era. From this standpoint, it will be necessary to (1) study the need for the social capital concerned, the requirement of a fair and steady supply of social capital, and the possibility of the supply of social capital through market mechanisms, and to keep a proper sharing of the burden between the government and the private sector: (2) open up the relationship between those who receive the benefits and those who bear the burden concerning semi-public assets and private assets, to re-study its significance and effect, and clarify the corresponding relations between those receiving the benefit and those who assume the role of providing it: (3) make a full study of the possibility of giving the private sector the responsibility of controlling and managing completed social capital.

Also, concerning the buildup in the nucleus of social capital, the state should assume responsibility for those matters related to the nation as a whole, and at the same time a basis should be established to stress the trend towards giving local authorities the responsibility and independence in dealing with matters of a local nature. A study also should be made on the undertaking of an effective buildup in social capital suited to people's needs by paying attention to the safety of economic society and the maintenance of a national minimum.

Furthermore, in order to seek an effective buildup in social capital, (1) attention must be paid to the mutual balance and connection between various sectors; (2) fully completed social capital should be put forward with due consideration to its future maintenance and control; (3) work should be conducted on the establishment of a new system and rules for effective undertakings designed to eliminate obstacles to the implementation of smooth management of the matters concerned, such as the acquisition of necessary land, payment of compensation or increases in land prices; (4) efforts must be made to promote technical development and save on construction costs; and (5) attempts should be made to make further use of analyses on the effect of costs.

## 3. The Role of the Public Sector and Proper Accommodatory Measures

(1)  Size of Government

The size of the Japanese government has so far been rather small on an international scale. It is appropriate to say that the Japanese government's financial and monetary systems have played proper roles in sustaining the growth of the nation's economy.

Namely, the government has played an important part in positively carrying out income tax reduction, keeping the nation's general account budget small, thereby establishing the framework of a system aimed at directing household savings into investment in private enterprises; in rectifying the balance derived from the high growth of the economy by implementing income redistribution involving farmers and small businesses; in supplying large funds at low interest rates in its financial loans to the nation's key undertakings, important industries, housing and living related facilities, and in building up social capital serving as the foundation for the development of economic society.

However, in connection with changes in the economic society in recent years, problems related to the effectiveness of the public sector and its rivalry with the private sector have been pointed out.

[The Possibility for Bigger Government]

When the size of a government is seen in terms of the total expenditure of general government in proportion to gross national product, Japan is at a relatively low level compared to other advanced countries, as cited in Table 3-4-2. From this standpoint, the Japanese government is small under the present circumstances.

However, there have been rapid increases in recent years in the percentage of the government's total general outlay occupying Japan's GNP. If it moves along at the present rate, there is the strong possibility

## Table 3-4-2  The Scope of Government

### (1) An International Comparison of the Scale of Government

(In %)

| Countries | Year | Ratio of total general government expenditures as against GNP | Ratio of tax burden (A) | Ratio of social security burden (B) | (A) + (B) |
|---|---|---|---|---|---|
| Japan | 1979 | 31.8 | 22.5 | 9.0 | 31.5 |
| U.S. | 1978 | 33.5 | 28.9 | 9.6 | 38.5 |
| Britain | 1979 | 43.1 | 39.3 | 9.7 | 49.0 |
| West Germany | 1979 | 44.3 | 32.6 | 19.6 | 52.2 |
| France | 1979 | 44.9 | 29.3 | 25.3 | 54.6 |
| Sweden | 1979 | 61.6 | 45.1 | 19.0 | 64.1 |

Notes:

1. **Sources:** Economic Planning Agency "Annual Report on National Accounts"; OECD "National Accounts of OECD Countries."

2. The years for Japan are fiscal years; those for other countries are calendar years.

3. The tax and social security burden ratios are compared with the national income.

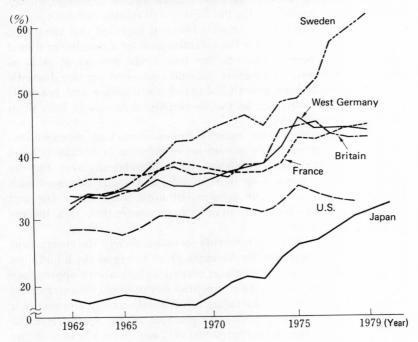

of Japan having a big government comparable in size to European nations in the near future.

Looking at the experiences of the United States and Western European countries, an excess increase in the scope of the public sector leads to rivalry with the private sector; rises in the burden of taxes etc. of the public sector; a distortion in the distribution of resources; a decline in the effectiveness of the public sector, and declines in incentives in the private sector (a lessening of desires to work and save). Consequently, there is the possibility of a fall in the vitality of economic society.

(2)   New Roles to Cope with the Changes in Economic Society

On the other hand, in the midst of progress in "internationalization," "the aging society" and the "maturity" of economic society, there is the expectation for the public sector to assume new roles.

In coping with internationalization, it is expected that the public sector will have to strive for the establishment of a new international economic structure based on the free trade system as well as international rules; to promote measures to open up the domestic market; to implement smooth industrial coordination and positively expand official assistance to the developing countries to help them develop their economies.

The government also must maintain economic management, attaching importance to the prevention of inflation in dealing with the aging society. It should establish a system allowing the aged and the handicapped to participate in economic and social activities with freedom from anxiety. The government must work out a fair and effective social security system in order to guarantee them their income and preserve their health.

In accommodating the maturing economic society, the government should promote technical development which serves as the foundation for the vitality of economic society; check stagflation with appropriate economic policies; maintain a competitive environment for enterprises; make efforts to preserve the safety of economic society and secure a steady supply of energy resources; promote energy saving and the development of alternative energy sources, and press ahead with the stockpiling of oil.

Another role the government is likely to be asked to assume involves the steady accumulation of effective and quality social capital befitting the demands of an era that will have to cope with the changes in economic society.

### (3)   A New Look at the Public Sector and Its Effectiveness

As seen above, the role the public sector is likely to play in future will be diversified. In order for it to take proper charge of its role, it will be necessary to take a new look at the ideal way for it to be and seek its effectiveness. At that time, it will also be necessary to realize that in a free economic society, the basis of the public sector is to support, guide and assist the private sector in its activities; to constantly consider not obstructing the activities of the private sector, and to realize anew its role which is to provide a framework for free and active economic and social activities.

## [The Need for a New Look]

With respect to the need for a new look at the ideal existence of the public sector, the following two points deserve a special mention.

First, amidst medium economic growth, the need has arisen for a new look at the measures considered proper during the era of high economic growth. That is to say, it was possible to respond with relative ease to various financial demands by expanding the scale of finances in tune with the expansion of the economy at the time of high economic growth. However, it is difficult to uphold this kind of thinking after the nation has shifted to an era of medium economic growth. There is an increasing need for either positive improvement or abolition of the system which no longer answers the demands of the era.

Second, as already seen, increases in social security related costs in the midst of the aging society trend will become a major cause for expanding the government's financial scope. Depending on the way the system is, there is the possibility of it affecting the private sector's incentive and causing a loss of vitality in the economy.

## [The Effectiveness of Policy]

In order to seek effectiveness in the public sector, it is necessary not only to achieve efficiency in the actual means of implementing fixed measures (primary effectiveness) but also constantly check on whether the fixed measures are in tune with the needs of society and whether they are effective or not (secondary effectiveness). From this standpoint, it will be important to (1) expand the sunset formula and seek its effectiveness: (2) effectively implement a self-supporting accounting system: (3) search for the means to set a limit to the piling up of deficits. Efforts must be made concerning both private and semi-public assets (1) to make clear who those receiving the benefits and those bearing the burden are and collect appropriate compensation, (2) to take a new look at delivery in kind, and (3) to lower the rate of assistance and introduce market theory by shifting from subsidies to loans, guarantees and insurance.

From this standpoint, it will be necessary to take a renewed look at the government's outlays to local public bodies, its social security payments and investment in public works projects, and ensure that the public sector plays an appropriate role in response to the changes in economic society.

Also, from the standpoint of conducting effective administrative services befitting the needs of regional society, it will be necessary to make a long-term study on the further effective utilization of the independence of local public bodies.

## (4) The Formation of National Consensus on the Ideal Way of Assuming the Burden

Even 'if the above-mentioned measures are adopted to cope with future trends in Japan, the proportion of social security transfers in national income is expected to rise as we move into an era of maturity of the pension system and increases in medical costs of the aged. Thus, it will be inevitable for the nation to expand the scope of the public sector, including social security, from a long-term point of view, and increases in the burden of the people will be unavoidable.

However, considering various economic-social difficulties faced by the advanced Western European countries due to their expansion of the public sector, it will be necessary for Japan to prevent such a situation in advance and make the utmost efforts to keep the nation from falling into such difficulties.

Together with such efforts, it will be important that full debates be conducted among the people and that a consensus is reached on the forthcoming inevitable increases in their burden from a long-term point of view, and also on what kind of choice there will be for the relationship between those receiving the benefits and those bearing the burden.

# Conclusion

In this report, we have mentioned that there will be three major trends — progress in internationalization, the arrival of the aging society, and the maturity of economic society — as Japanese economic society undergoes changes. The following are the basic ideas on the means to cope with them.

First, Japan must realize the position it occupies in the world economy and become aware of the fact that the prosperity of the world is essential to its own existence. Japan should actively play its part in the stability and development of international communities and further internationalize its economic society.

Second, in order to prepare for the certain arrival of the aging society in the 21st century, Japan must take a renewed look at its existing systems and customs, work out new mechanisms, and steadily build up its social environment in order to realize a society comfortable for the people to live in.

Third, as economic society progresses towards maturity, efforts must be made to maintain and shape its vitality and display it. In order to do so, it will be necessary to move forward with technical innovation and reflect the results on society; to maintain the basic framework for a democratic and free economic society, and to recognize both diversified ways of life and sense of values for the sake of establishing a society in which each person can elevate his or her sense of participation.

The basic strategy towards the establishment of the aforementioned economic society must have the following:

There are three alternatives for the progress in internationalization:

(1)    Japan must positively strive to reactivate the world economy.

(2)    Japan must further open up its economic society to be acceptable internationally.

(3)    Japan must positively contribute to the settlement of various problems on a global scale, such as the North-South issue, and food and environmental problems.

The following five alternatives must be taken into account for the aging society.

Given the four doctrines — "a society allowing individuals to freely demonstrate their ability and also capable of responding to diversified needs," "a fair and balanced society," "a broad-minded society," and "a society capable of coping with progress in internationalization" — Japan must try:

(1) to continue economic management attaching importance to the prevention of inflation.

(2) to establish a society permitting the aged to make use of their valuable knowledge and experience, and their participation in economic and social activities.

(3) to revise its public pension system to provide effective and appropriate welfare services.

(4) to establish a living environment in which the people can live pleasantly.

(5) to properly fix the role of the home.

In order to cope with the maturity of economic society, and maintain and shape its vitality, the following three alternatives must be considered.

(1) Efforts must be made not only to develop both applied and improved technology, but also to develop individualistic and creative technology and train creative people.

(2) Efforts must be made to maintain a competitive environment for individuals and enterprises, to maintain the principle of enterprise organization and employment customs retaining special Japanese characteristics, in line with the changes of the times as well as to implement a proper economic policy so that the private sector can exhibit its vitality.

(3) In order to cope with diversification of the people's sense of values and consciousness, an environment for active cultural and social activities must be fully provided as must opportunities for pluralized self-realization.

Also, as something which is common to the three major trends, the following matters must also be tackled.

(1) More attention must be paid to the safety of economic society. Efforts should be made to pursue safety with mutual international reliance and also by building multiple safety facilities.

(2) Attempts should be made to realize a comfortable and open society for permanent settlement, while efforts must be made to systematically provide quality national land and living space for the

next generation to inherit.

(3)   Work on taking a new look at the public sector and making it more effective must be done so that it will be able to cope with the changes in economic society and properly carry out its role.

What has become clear through our study made so far is that in the next 20 years going into the 21st century, Japanese economic society will face an extremely important period for its future. It is no exaggeration to say that the future of our country will be considerably affected depending on how we cope with that period.

In the international community, the world economy is expected to become multipolarized in future but moves for its stability will also continue. In the midst of this situation, there is a strong possibility that Japan's status will continue to rise. Japan is likely to be asked to play more roles and assume further responsibilities in the international community. Thus, the next 20 years will be a period in which Japan must carry out its duty and press ahead with genuine internationalization of its economic society.

Japan will certainly have an aging society in the 21st century. It will surpass even the present standard of advanced Western European nations, as it will be the most longevous society in history. The next 20 years will be an important period for us to prepare for those problems expected to come up in future.

Looking at its development stage, it is believed that Japanese economic society will enter a process of maturity in future. As the people's perception of life changes and their way of life becomes diversified, there will be a number of signs of change in the vitality of Japanese economic society. The period under review will be a period necessary for maintaining the vitality of economic society and demonstrating the same in resolving various problems both at home and abroad in the process of maturity.

Fortunately, Japan will continue to have a high population percentage of people of productive age. And, although it is expected that the people's savings ratio will fall, it will still be higher than that of Western European nations. The Japanese people are being given the opportunity to display their power in accordance with their abilities. Enterprises with maintain the framework of a free economy which can develop through their own creative devices and competition. Whether or not such an economic society will be able to fully demonstrate its power by maintaining its basic framework will be the key to the settling of various problems.

The course our economic society will take in future will not necessarily be even. A number of difficulties and obstacles will stand in its way. Time will be needed to revise the system, the mechanisms and the practices of the economic society in coping with the new situation. In this sense, the next 20 years will be an important period. The time available in some cases may not be enough, but it will still be enough if we start now to prepare for the 21st century.

The path our economic society treads will differ depending on the choice we make now.

What is important is that we must pass on an economic society full of vitality, which will not leave any heavy burden for future generations to bear. For this purpose, it will be necessary to foster people armed with both the desire to work and compassion, and develop social characteristics which will encourage people to use their wisdom in conquering difficulties. We must prepare now for the establishment of such a society so that the next generation will be able to inherit it. This is the duty of we who live in the present age.